THE VISITOR'S GUID1
THE TYROL

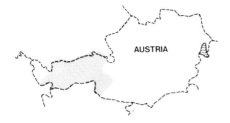

AUSTRIA

Visitor's Guide Series

This series of guide books gives, in each volume, the details and facts needed to make the most of a holiday in one of the tourist areas of Britain and Europe. Not only does the text describe the country-side, villages, and towns of each region, but there is also valuable information on where to go and what there is to see. Each book includes, where appropriate, stately homes, gardens and museums to visit, nature trails, archaeological sites, sporting events, steam railways, cycling, walking, sailing, fishing, country parks, useful addresses — everything to make your visit more worthwhile.

Other titles already published or planned include:
The Lake District (revised edition)
The Peak District (revised edition)
The Chilterns
The Cotswolds
North Wales
The Yorkshire Dales
Cornwall
Devon
East Anglia
Somerset and Dorset
Guernsey, Alderney and Sark
The Scottish Borders
   and Edinburgh
The Welsh Borders
Historic Places of Wales
The North York Moors, York and
   the Yorkshire Coast
South and West Wales
Kent
Hampshire and The Isle of Wight
Sussex
Dordogne (France)
Brittany (France)
Black Forest (W Germany)
The South of France
Loire
French Coast

KEY FOR MAPS

● Towns - Villages

━━━ Main Roads

Rivers

†††††† Railways

Lakes/Reservoirs

Ⅲ Museum/Art
Gallery/Centre

▲ Archaeological Site

❷ Wildlife Park/Zoo
Sanctuary

Ħ Castle/Fort

✿ Other Place of Interest

The Visitor's Guide To
THE TYROL

Alan Proctor

MOORLAND PUBLISHING

HUNTER
PUBLISHING INC.

British Library Cataloguing in
Publication Data

Proctor, Alan
    The Visitor's Guide to the Tyrol
    1. Tyrol (Austria) — Description
    and travel — Guide-books
    I. Title
    914.36′420453   DB769.2

Acknowledgements

Black and white illustrations have been
supplied by the Austrian National Tourist
Office. Colour illustrations have been
supplied by H. Alcock (Heiligenblut, Gross
Glockner); Austrian National Tourist Office
(Lermoos, Mayrhofen, St Leonhard); G.
Webster (Montafon); the remainder were
supplied by the author.

Published by
Moorland Publishing Co Ltd,
8 Station Street,
Ashbourne, Derbyshire,
DE6 1DE England.
Tel: (0335) 44486

ISBN 0 86190 128 2 (paperback)
ISBN 0 86190 129 0 (hardback)

Published in the USA by
Hunter Publishing Inc,
300 Raritan Center Parkway,
CN94, Edison, NJ 08818

ISBN 0 935161 42 2 (paperback)

Printed in the UK by
Butler and Tanner Ltd,
Frome, Somerset.

Contents

Preface

Austria probably has more variety to offer than any other European country. The towns seem to have a timeless air about them, the villages step right out of the picture postcards.

Travelling about the country brings one face to face with a culture developed over centuries. Many imposing castles, survivors of the middle ages, dominate valleys from the higher ground. Frequently they have been changed into hotels or restaurants where the tourist is made welcome.

The welcome is always kind, smiling and sincere. Tourists are never made to feel that they are intruders, and if they want to stop and take part in the life of the community the welcome is a happy one. Folklore is especially strong in the Tyrol, and in the evenings many establishments have a folk event. This may be two or three people with zither and guitar; however, there are almost always songs in which the tourist are invited to join.

The abbeys and parish churches, mostly Baroque, are brilliant examples of religious art.

Above all tower the imposing mountains, many of which carry snow all year round. Two thirds of Austria is mountainous, in summer a paradise for walkers and in winter a paradise for skiers. For the latter the Tyrol is most popular, but most of the chair lifts and cable cars operate all year round, so that the summer walker can swiftly be transported to the heights.

THE TYROL

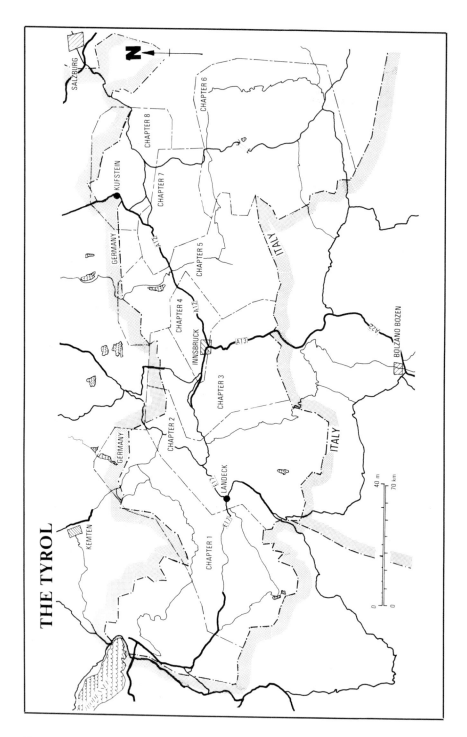

Introduction

The youngest, and possibly the most thriving, industry in Austria is tourism. The genuine friendliness of the people is evident for all to see. One may meet the zither player from last night's entertainment going about his everyday job; he will take time to greet people, shake hands and wish you a happy holiday, all with a beaming smile.

Music is of prime importance and though the tourist may not be able to visit the opera every village has its quota of entertainments. These range from a single quiet zither player, a group of yodellers, to a full scale Tyrolean dance troupe. A Tyrolean evening with a shoe platter group is a delight, and the visitors may well be drawn into the dancing.

Village festivals occur at frequent intervals; they are a great favourite with tourists and a photographer's paradise. Yet they are a part of the life of the village, not a display. The clergy, the village dignitaries, firemen and rifle brigade, all dressed in traditional costume, are a delight to the eye. Processions are followed by villagers, all proudly maintaining centuries of tradition.

Food and drink are taken seriously in Austria. With such a rich historical past they have adopted and Austrianized dishes from other countries. The visitor can experiment with the menu without fear. No fiery concoctions will attack the palate or stomach. However, it may be advisable to watch one's waistline. Austrians like food, and portions tend to be large and filling. They eat well and often.

Restaurants, coffee shops and the ubiquitous guest houses all have one thing in common; their excellent service. There is never any hurry; sit and wait until the waiter comes, and with a gracious *bitte sehr* your order will be taken. The next problem is paying, as there is never a suggestion that you should drink up and go. Your beer or coffee can last all evening if you wish. Trying to catch the waiter's eye to pay can take quite a time. A gentle *Zahlen Bitte* as he goes by is the best way.

One of the most civilised things, to me, is for a family to be able to have a break, the children with an ice cream, and either coffee or a glass of beer for the adults, all at the same table, and at any time of day. The Austrians have a word for it, *gemütlichkeit*, which embraces the jovial happy atmosphere.

To describe a town or village as picturesque or pretty in Austria is to declare it outstanding. Almost all the towns and villages are decorative. Every house has window boxes and balconies filled with flowers. Many houses have delightful mural paintings.

From the very earliest times Austria has been a pageant of people on the move. The Romans conquered it, and kept a road through the Alps open all year round, quite a feat even today at the higher levels. Armies, traders and settlers came and went; Goths, the Vandals, Attila the Hun, Teutons, Slavs, Franks and Burgundians. They were followed by the Magyars of Hungary who devastated the country until they were defeated by the Franks and Bavarians. In AD800 Charlemagne was crowned Emperor by the Pope. But the mighty empire he built, which included Austria, was divided after his death.

At the end of the thirteenth century the House of Hapsburg came to rule over Austria. Their rule continued until 1918. Between those times they survived the plots, intrigues and wars which raged round Europe and their empire. Most important of these wars, perhaps, was the two-hundred-year struggle against the Turks waged by Austria during the sixteenth and seventeenth centuries, culminating in a massive Turkish defeat and the preservation of a Christian Europe. In this period Austria became the centre of the counter-reformation.

Early in the eighteenth century one of the greatest queens of history came to the throne. Maria Theresa was a great reformer. She gathered the feudal states together under a central adminstration, and reformed trade, education and the church. Her reign was a golden era for cultural expansion, as this was the age of Haydn and Mozart, and high Baroque in art and architecture.

Napoleon transformed the Europe of his day; amongst other things, he defeated the German princes and humiliated them by placing them under his own authority. He subsequently married an Austrian princess in an attempt to stabilise his position in Europe.

The next great figure to arise was Bismark. He wished to unite Germany under one rule, dominated by Prussia but excluding Austria. In 1866 Bismark, along with his new ally Italy, atacked Austria. The Austrians defeated the Italians but were in turn beaten by Bismark at Sadowa in Bohemia.

In 1914 World War I brought disaster and disintegration to the Hapsburg Empire. At the end of the war the Republic of Austria was brought into being, consisting of the German speaking part of the Empire. The Magyars, Poles, Croats, Czechs, Slovaks and other unwilling subjects of the Hapsburgs created new countries for themselves, rejecting Austrian domination. This period of Austria's history was a disaster. What had been built up as a great empire, with lines of communication centred on Vienna, was now only a tiny remnant. Produce was cut off from its markets, and ports from their hinterland. Financial chaos and hyper-inflation raged.

Chancellor Dolfuss took office in 1932 and turned his one-party rule into a dictatorship in 1934, following a five-day civil war. Dolfuss feared the Nazis who had proclaimed plans to incor-porate Austria into Germany. After parliament was dissolved in 1934 the Nazis unsuccessfully tried to start a civil war. Dolfuss was murdered and his successor, Schuschnigg, could not resist the pressure, and in March 1938, German troops marched unopposed into Austria. Eighteen months later World War II began.

In May 1945 Austria was occupied by the Russians, then by the French, American and British forces. Though many troops had retired earlier, a peace treaty was not signed until May 1955.

Modern Austria is a democratic federal republic divided into nine federal states. She holds a respected position in international affairs, lending active support to the work of the United Nations. Austria sent troops to Cyprus, and medical teams to assist the cause of world peace.

Austria is very easy to reach. One may take the car ferry to Vlissingen or Ostend, then the German motorways by way of Cologne. Another route is through northern France via Strasbourg and Lake Constance. The fastest way is via German motorways and, for the time-conscious traveller it is possible to drive from the outskirts of Ostend almost to the Austrian border without leaving the motorway.

Before reaching the Tyrol from Lake Constance one passes through the Vorarlberg. This region is almost cut off from the rest of Austria by the Arlberg Pass, and once almost became a part of a Switzerland. Over the Arlberg Pass, now an all-weather road, the long descent into the Tyrol begins. The mighty River Inn is reached at Landeck and runs along the valley to Kufstein, where it enters Germany. The Inn rises in Switzerland to the south of the Silvretta range which forms the border, and crosses the border with Austria into the Tyrol near Nauders. Between Nauders and Ried is the Oberinntal (Higher Inn Valley). The tourist authority claims, as a scientific fact, that here the sun shines longer and more brightly than anywhere else.

This long main valley runs easterly, then north-east nearer Kufstein. Also running north-east from the Arlberg is the famous Lechtal (Lech Valley). Both the Lech and the Inn run into the Danube and eventually into the Black Sea.

Reaching out from the main valley are side valleys; some are dead ends as far as the motorist is concerned, some like the Wipp Tal carry main routes. This one leads to the Brenner Pass, now crossed by a motorway.

Eastward the next major valleys lie just beyond Jenbach. North is the Achental which carries a main road over the Achen-pass into Germany. The road runs between the Karwendel mountains and the Rofan group. On the main valley is the beautiful Achensee, a long narrow lake, and a favourite spot for wind-surfers. South of Jenbach is the Zillertal. Near the head of the valley is Zell am Ziller, and at this point a road goes left to climb up into the lovely hanging Gerlos valley. This road then continues over the Gerlos Pass (507 metres) and into Salzburg Province.

Higher up the valley is Mayrhofen, which stands at the confluence of four

---

TRAVEL BY CAR

Car Ferry Routes
Dover or Folkestone to Ostend or Dunkirk by Sealink. Dover or Felixstowe to Zeebrugge by Townsend Thorensen. Sheerness to Vlissingen by Olau Lines. All quickly join the continental motorway system. Harwich to the Hook of Holland is another Sealink service. US and UK tourists need only a valid driving licence and the car log book, though you are still advised to obtain a 'Green Card' international insurance card before leaving home, otherwise you are only covered by third-party insurance. This comes from your own insurance company.

In Austria
Safety belts must be worn. Children under twelve are not allowed in front seats.

Speed Limits
Motorways: 130km/hr (80mph). Main roads: 100km/hr (63mph). Built up areas: 50km/hr (35mph). Trailers over ¾ ton — Motorways: 70km/hr (45mph); main roads: 60km/hr (40mph). On steep gradients remember to engage a low gear early. The vehicle travelling uphill always has priority. Many of the high passes are not recommended for, or are closed to, caravans.

ACCOMMODATION

Hotels

This is the most expensive and most luxurious way to stay.

Gasthof

German for country hotel, of moderate size with a good restaurant, often indistinguishable from a hotel.

Gasthaus

A country inn, often the emphasis is on food and drink, but most have beds.

Pension

Often called a *Frühstücks-Pension*, a guest-house offering bed and breakfast only.

Last on the list in descending order of expense is a private room, with breakfast. Any house with a sign *Zimmer* (room) offers this service. It will be cheap, clean and comfortable, with the usual coffee and rolls breakfast.

There is an extensive network of camping and caravan sites. Anyone who is a member of Youth Hostels Association can take advantage of the Austrian Youth Hostels, all excellent and near or in delightful holiday centres.

For something different try an Austrian farmhouse. For families with children they are economical, picturesque and very pleasant, mostly offering bed and breakfast only. The Austrian National Tourist Office will provide a list.

Castle Hotels are the old castles, many of them historic, which have been converted into luxury hotels. Again the Tourist Office will provide a list.

valleys coming down from the Zillertal Alps.

Over the Gerlos Pass and down to Mittersill a main road goes south to the Felbertauern Tunnel. This three-mile long tunnel has opened up the beautiful valleys of the East Tyrol to tourists. The road is open all year round.

A road goes down to Lienz before swinging east then north into Carinthia for one of the most spectacular drives of the whole area. From here one may travel north to the spectacular village of Heiligenblut, which lies on the south slope of the Grossglockner. From Heiligenblut it is forty-seven miles to Zell am See, over the toll road which reaches, 2,428 metres (7,964ft).

At Zell am See turn back west to Mittersill, then north to Kitzbühel which is a very picturesque winter and summer resort.

From Kitzbühel head for Wörgl, back in the main Inn valley, touring gently upstream to Brixlegg and Münster before returning and going on to Kufstein. From here short expeditions can be made to the beautiful lake of Thiersee and round the Kaiser Gebirge (Emperor Mountains) to St Johann in Tyrol, Walschsee and back to Kufstein.

All this is at the eastern end of the Tyrol. In the west the route makes a spectacular entry into the province by way of the Silvretta Strasse. Leave the motorway at Bludenz and take the toll road towards Partenen and Galtür. It is almost sixty miles to Landeck. Caravans are not allowed and there is a toll. The ascent has thirty hairpin bends and starts by following the Montafon valley. Schruns is soon reached; it lies at 689 metres, and the summit of the pass is 2,036 metres.

From Landeck it is possible to turn back to cross the Arlberg Pass, but it is better to turn north near the summit to

Zürs and Lech. Lech is at the head of the Lechtal, and the River Lech can be followed down to Reutte before coming east again to Ehrwald, a delightful village.

The Fernpass, a delightful valley full of beautiful lakes, leads once more into the main Inn valley at Imst. From Landeck over the Arlberg to Reutte and back to Imst the route has completely encompassed the Lechtaler Alps.

The next chapters will give details of this area. Do not worry about language difficulties; English is spoken by many of the people, it is taught in the schools as the primary foreign language from the age of seven onwards. If the waiter or garage hand cannot understand you he will quickly call someone who can, even if it means calling the chef out of the kitchen.

Of course, the larger establishments always make a point of having an English-speaking receptionist. If in doubt ask; the friendly Austrians delight in being able to explain, or practise their English. Be it the menu or the best path to take to a view-point, a friendly, cheerful response is assured.

In the further information section towns and villages with tourist offices are listed. It is almost impossible to list all the varied and minor evening entertainments. Some only operate in the high season. For instance, at Ehrwald there is a music show with old traditional instruments, but only in the school holidays. Again many hotels have an evening of folk music. The local tourist office will have up to date times, dates and venues. Should you have trouble getting a room the local tourist office will help.

Many resorts offer a walk programme. A sketch map of the paths in the area is obtained from the local tourist office. Stamps are collected in a 'walker's pass' at a number of places on route. These enable gold, silver, bronze and even 'alpine' badges to be won (and paid for!).

The local tourist offices may also organise a free 'photo-safari' or a wild flower tour, but as details vary enquire locally on arrival.

Walks are indicated by a vertical line in the margin with approximate milages and times for each walk. Also there is a severity guide which is:

*   =   Easy
**   =   Moderate
***   =   Hard

1 The Arlberg and Lechtal

The Tyrol is reached at the Bielerhöhe Pass, altitude 2,036 metres, on the Tyrolean side of the Paznaun Valley which runs north-east. Where the main valley is jointed a left turn takes the route back westerly up to the Arlberg Pass on the main road number 316.

Crossing the Arlberg back into the region of Vorarlberg is the most convenient route into the famous Lechtal, via the town of Lech, where the river Lech is joined. The route continues down the magnificent Lechtal to Reutte, almost on the German border. From Reutte it is possible to cross the border into Germany to visit the castles at Schwangau. There are two campsites on a lakeside setting, and two castles. Hohenschwangau is the original castle which was a home. Neuschwanstein is the fairytale castle built by Ludwig of Bavaria. Its interior was never completed as Ludwig met a sad end, drowned in the nearby lake. However, the exterior is a fantastic sight. Some of the interior was finished.

The spires and turrets make a fascinating sight when viewed either from the valley or from higher up the many paths through the woods. Car parking is in the valley, and the walk up the driveway takes almost half an hour. There are horse drawn conveyances which travel almost to the top. English speaking guides are available on request at no extra cost.

From an approach past Lake Constance through Lindau and Bregenz take the motorway to Bludenz and follow it until the signs for Schruns appear. Leave the motorway and take the road into the Montafon Valley, signposted Partenen and Galtür. The Silvretta Road is closed to caravans, no doubt due to its thirty hairpin bends and four thousand feet of ascent. However, it is possible to camp in the main valley and tour the Silvretta Road, returning over the Arlberg.

From Bludenz to Landeck is about sixty miles, with the summit of the pass being reached about half-way. The road is generally closed by snow from November to May and has a toll which is collected beyond Partenen.

The Montafon valley is very pleasant and quite heavily populated. Tschagguns and Schruns, within a mile of each other, are the first places reached. The ancient village centre of Schruns offers a very pleasant stroll, and the Dorfstrasse is closed to motor traffic, enhancing a visit. Having a population of almost four thousand, this is the main town of the valley. It is not a fashionable place in the tourist sense, but has some good skiing in the winter and splendid views of the Rätikon group to the west. Both are winter and summer resorts.

Just before the next town there is a turning south to Gargellen, a tiny Alpine village at 1,480 metres, and a winter and summer resort. St Gallenkirch is a picturesque town of almost two thousand inhabitants, with the usual winter facilities. Gaschurn is the next little place on route, a popular winter sport resort. Local guides will take parties on mountaineering or skiing tours on the Silvretta or Ferwall. The less enthusiastic can fish, ride or just stroll through the woods of the lower

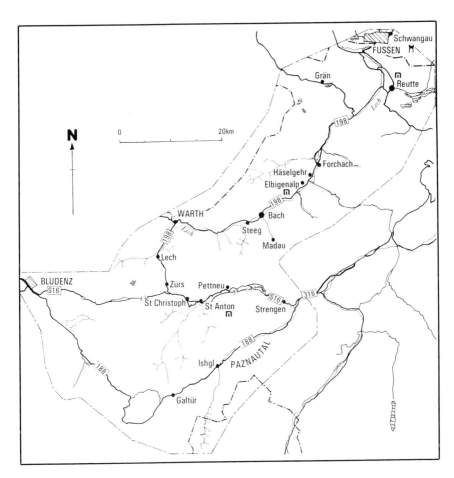

slopes on the network of footpaths.

The valley now has a more alpine look and from the next village, which is Partenen, the ascent proper begins. Partenen is a pleasant village, lying at 1,050 metres, and there is a good skiing. Just beyond the village the Silvretta High Alpine Road begins; actually it is a private road belonging to the power company, and there is a toll. Twenty-four kilometres of curves and bends climb 1,000 metres to the Bielerhöhe Pass at 2,036 metres (6,700ft).

One of the large power plants is at Partenen, with another higher up the valley. Water is piped down from the lakes and dams at considerable pressure due to the height. Both plants were opened before World War II but enlarged afterwards when artificial lakes were built.

Vermunt-Stausee is the first lake, at 1,743 metres, and allows a pause in the climb. The summit of the pass, the Bielerhöhe, at 2,036 metres (6,680ft) is a natural stopping place. A large hotel is a base for mountain expeditions and for spring skiing in the Silvretta Mountains. It is possible to walk along the crest of the dam, which is 431 metres long and 80 metres high. The mountain peaks to the south form the border with Switzerland;

15

Climb to the Fluchthorn, Ischgl

the highest mountain in view is the Piz Buin, 3,316 metres high.

Here on the eastern shore of the lake is the border with the Tyrol. Downhill to the east is the grassy dell of Klein-vermunt leading down to the Paznaun valley and the Trisanna river. Galtür is the first hamlet, with a population of less than seven hundred, but there are five winter chair lifts and an indoor swimming pool. For an alpine walk from Galtür go south of the village up the Jamtal. Involving 332 metres of ascent it is a good safe walk up to the Jamtalhütte, an alpine hut, more like an inn. Return the same way. The time required to reach the hut is about two and a half hours. There is parking space at the Scheibalm. The Alpine system of giving times for walks will be adhered to in this guide. Distance is not really relevant to an alpine walk, as the ground varies so much and rougher tracks take

longer times. Times given are for average walkers and allow time for short breaks for taking in the views and for photography. Remember that this is mountain country, ask your over-night host for advice regarding the weather if in doubt. A good idea is to carry a small rucksack with a sweater and waterproofs. Bad weather in the Alps usually comes later in the day, so make an early start.

The next village down the Paznauntal is Ischgl and it is below the tree line, which started on the way down from Galtür. Built on a slight spur and below the village church it is most attractive. It is the largest village in the valley, lies at 1,377 metres, and is regarded as a health resort in summer; it is, of course, a skiing centre in winter; fishing and riding are also available. Both the villages have tourist offices at which to check exact locations and times.

**

Galtür
Mountain walk. Indoor swimming pool.

Ischgl
Mountain walk. Cable car. Fishing. Riding. Swimming.

Picturesque Villages
Kappl. Langesthei. See Trissana Bridge.

On a bus route.

**

There is a cable car which can quickly whisk one to a height of 2,612 metres. At this height, walk slowly. It is possible to walk down. Follow the track south then east from the mountain station of the cable car. This track joins footpath No. 715 to the Velillscharte *(scharte:*fissure) 2,556 metres. The walk should take three-quarters-of-an-hour. This good path goes down the Velilltal to join a road before the village. Total time for walking is two and a half hours, walking easily.

Another interesting walk from Ischgl is across the Swiss border to the Heidelberger Hut , at 2,264 metres. Drive up the Fimbertal to the Gh Bodenalpe, at 1,842 metres, then walk up the good track. There are no border formalities. Time required is four hours, easy going. Once across the Swiss border the valley becomes the Val Fenga, an attractive valley surrounded by peaks almost 10,000ft high. There is a bus service from Landeck up the main valley to Galtür.

**

There are three more villages on the way down the valley. They are picturesque, perched on terraces to catch the sun. Woods become denser and the road still follows the torrent of the river. A glimpse ahead of Wiesberg Castle

Village view, Ischgl

17

marks the end of the valley. The castle is at one end of the famous Trisanna Bridge, *Trisannabrucke,* a railway bridge of light and slender metal which adds great attraction and strength to the view from its height of 82 metres above the foaming river.

Now the route goes back to the west, up to the Arlberg Pass. The first hamlet is Strengen which lies in a ravine, and the next is Flirsch which lies in pastureland. This variation is part of the charm of the route. This is the Stanzertal. Be sure to follow the signs for St Christoph am Arlberg, as the new main road takes the Arlberg Tunnel. Pettneu is a charming little village set safely back off the main road, a nearby church has a memorial to the tunnellers who died constructing the Arlberg Tunnel.

Part of the charm of this valley is the geography. Wide meadows lie to the south of Pettneu with woods to the north. Behind the woods rise the massive limestone crags of the Lechtaler Alps, showing very pale in the bright sunshine. South are the snowy heights of the Hohe Riffler with the peaks glistening with snow.

St Anton on the Arlberg is next, a name to lift the hearts of dedicated skiers. It is on a main railway route, the famous Arlberg Express stops here, so access is easy. Alpine skiing was devised and taught here as early as 1901. An Austrain named Hannes Schneider developed the method. In 1926 he made a film, 'The Wonders of Skiing', which was a tremendous success. Arnold Lunn, the founder of the British Kandahar Ski Club, introduced slalom gates to skiing in 1922. In 1927 the two men met and their collaboration resulted in the first Arlberg-Kandahar Cup Race in St Anton in 1928.

The ski runs are mostly above the tree line, but this does not mean there is nothing to do in summer. There are nearby woodland walks, fishing and mountain walks. A chair lift goes up, in two stages, to 2,333 metres, and a cable car goes up to the Valluga, at 2,809 metres. There is a tourist information office in the town to check all the latest details.

For the energetic there are plenty of walks. The two-stage chair lift has its middle station at Gampen, where there is a mountain restaurant and a signposted walk back down through the woods to the town. For a longer, more exciting, walk take the chair lift to the top station, the Kapall House, at 2,333 metres. Follow the path north from the hut then take the right fork. There are red marks on the rocky path to follow. In one-and-a-quarter hours the path reaches the Leutkircher Hut, 2,252 metres, following the national path No. 601. This is a high level path, part of the Lechtaler High Footpath *Lechtaler Hohenweg.* Path No. 642 goes back to St Anton, total time three-and-a-quarter hours.

From St Anton continue the climb to the pass summit, at 1,771 metres. St Christoph is just before the summit proper. A hospice was built in 1386.

THINGS TO DO IN STANZERTAL AND ARLBERG

Pettnau
Picturesque village.

St Anton
Mountain walk, fishing, riding, bowling, tennis hall, heated outdoor pool.

St Christoph
Hospice chapel.

On a bus route and railway line.

Mountains in winter from St Anton on Arlberg

Unfortunately this was burnt down in 1957 and the new building is the Hospice Hotel. Only part of the original chapel remains, and is joined on to the hotel. Visitors may peer into the chapel through a special viewing window.

Buses cross the pass on the Bludenz to Landeck route and also run up the Flexenpath road to Lech.

Approximately one mile on the Vorarlberg side of the pass, take the right fork to the Flexenpass and on to Lech. This is actually back in the Vorarlberg. From the first sharp bend there is a magnificent view, over the first tiny hamlet of Stuben just below, down the Klostertal with the peaks of the Rätikon Mountains in the distance. Climbing up towards the pass the road clings to the side of the mountain and required the building of almost three-quarters of a mile of galleries to protect

the road from avalanches. This road is kept open all year round as over the pass is the tiny hamlet of Zurs.

The valley widens just before Zurs is reached. Most of the big hotels will be closed until November when the snow arrives, and with the snow, the thousands of skiers. This treeless sunny valley boasts no less than eleven ski tows. One chair lift, in two stages, goes up to 2,702 metres. It will soon be possible to travel from Zurs to St Anton by cable car, making three changes and walking almost a quarter of a mile through a tunnel at an altitude of 2,581 metres. This is an exciting, though expensive, trip giving splendid high alpine views. This small valley is a paradise of Alpine flowers in summer, while in winter there may be anything from six to sixteen feet of snow.

A gentle slope leads down from Zürs

THINGS TO DO ROUND LECH

Lech
Riverside walk, heated swimming
pool, fishing.

On a bus route.

to Lech. Although it is argued that Zurs
is more fashionable as a ski resort Lech
is a genuine, and very pretty, village at
1,447 metres. Lech has more facilities
than Zurs and a network of chair lifts
and cable cars. It is possible to take a
cable car in Lech to the Rufikopf, at
2,350 metres. Ski down to Zurs, where
there is a double chair lift to the
Madlochjoch, 2,438 metres. Then it is
possible to ski down the Stierloch to Zug
and back to Lech.

Summer visitors will find a lovely
riverside walk from the southern end of
the village. Take the road, then the
footpath, to the south of the river. There
is a heated swimming pool half a mile
along. The path leads along the beautiful
upper Lech valley to Zug, where there is
a bridge over the river to the village.
This is a low level riverside walk of just
over a mile-and-a-half. The path
continues along the south side of the
river, for the more energetic, for another
mile-and-a-half. A bridge takes a track
over the river to the road. This road is a
dead end so there is little traffic, other
than holidaymakers visiting the upper
reaches of the valley.

The road to Warth is fairly level and
the distance is about five miles. Warth is
a small village in a beautiful mountain
setting. Here the road turns right
towards Reutte. Soon the River Lech is
in view again. This stretch of road,
Warth to Reutte, is an interesting
touring road. It has made its name as a
haven of peace. Quite away from the
bustle of the main touring centres, it is

an area where many will want to linger.

To the south tower the majestic
Lechtaler Alps. Though quieter it has a
great deal to offer. To really get the feel
of the Alps go up one of the side valleys
to the mountain villages: Madau south
of Bach, Gramais south of Häselgehr,
Hinterhornbach via Vorderhornbach
west of Stanzach, or Namlos to the east.

The valley has numerous hotels, inns
and pensions. It is possible just to relax,
to stroll gently through the meadows, or
to aim for the higher regions. For
example, from the mountain village of
Madau it is possible, on a good path, to
climb up to the Memminger Hut, at
2,242 metres (almost 7,000ft). Good
mountain walkers can go beyond up to
the three summits of the Zee kopf. The
summits are a scramble and are all about
2,700 metres in altitude.

Down in the valley there is the 'High
Green Footpath' from the village of
Bach to Häselgehr. There are at least
three swimming pools in the area and
facilities for many other sports including
climbing.

The mighty Alps dominate the scenery
with the Allgäuer Alps to the north-
west. However, the eye is constantly
drawn back to the river, this powerful
giant may be in gentle mood in the
summer season. Large areas of flood

IN THE LECHTAL

Holzgau
Local museum opening 1984.

Elbigenalp
Small museum at the Tourist Office.
Daily: 9-12am and 2-5pm.

Swimming pools at: Holzgau, Bach,
Häselgehr, Vorderhornbach and
Forchach.

Main valley road is on a bus route.

20

wash silently demonstrate the rise of water in the spring thaw. When all the side streams are in spate the power and noise of the main river is awesome.

In the pretty village of Elbigenalp there is a small professional wood carving school where the Tyrolean tradition of wood carving is maintained. Alongside the main church, which is seventeenth century and stands in fields slightly apart from the village, is the fifteenth-century Chapel of St Martin. The crypt once served as a charnel house and there are painted panels in the chapel representing the Dance of the Dead.

At Weissenbach there is an interesting side valley, the Tannheimer, on road No 199, and a lakeside campsite at the Haldensee. The valley is a famous beauty spot, and claimed to be one of the most beautiful in Europe. The road then leads on to Reutte. This town has a population of over five thousand and is the administrative and tourist capital of the Ausserfern. The Ausserfern is so called because it is, as the name implies, 'beyond the Fern', the Fern in this case being the Fern Pass, a mountain pass cutting off the area from the main Inn valley. Reutte is a pleasant town and a convenient centre for a few days' exploration. In keeping with the area there are some colourfully painted houses and an interesting small museum.

From Reutte take the road towards Füssen to visit the Lech Falls where the mighty river tumbles down onto the Bavarian plain. There is a small layby and a viewing platform. Then it is possible to continue to Schwangau and visit the two castles described earlier.

A minor road goes from Reutte to Plansee where there are campsites. Or it is possible to drive along the 314 road to Heiterwang, where the main road

Berwang

ROUND ABOUT REUTTE

Reutte
Picturesque town museum. Alpine
flower garden.

Schwangau
Two castles (in Germany).

Lech Falls
Near Füssen.

Heiterwang and Plansee
Picturesque lakes.

Holiday plane trips round the Alps,
guided walks, beauty farm, mountain
railway, swimming, riding, tennis.

HEITERWANG, PLANSEE

Riding, fishing, boat trips,
swimming, tennis, minigolf and
windsurfing

Heiterwang end. Anyone becoming tired
can take a ride part of the way back.
Plansee is the larger of the two lakes,
nearly six kilometres long.

Just outside Reutte is a mountain
railway taking visitors to a height of
almost 2,000 metres, where there is a
fascinating Alpine flower garden and the
'Alpine Rose Path' for a pleasant stroll.
Or there is the cable car to the Höfener
Alm which opens up a delightful
network of paths with fantastic
mountain views.

Beyond Heiterwang the road
undulates before gently descending to
Lermoos.

HALDENSEE

Swimming, sailing, boating, bowling,
windsurfing.

bypasses the village. There is a campsite
on the Heiterwang See as well. The two
lakes are joined by a narrow canal. An
easy day's walk is available from any
point round both lakes. Fascinating
views unfold as the walker proceeds.
Probably it is better to start from
Heiterwang and walk the eastern bank
of both lakes. This is because from the
head of Plansee a motorboat service
operates to the centre point and then
back to Hotel Fischer am See at the

2 Ehrwald, the Upper Inn and the Southerly Valleys

The main 314 road goes from Reutte to Imst and is joined by the 187 to Lermoos. This routes comes in from Germany and Garmisch-Partenkirchen, a very picturesque town.

Trains run regularly from Reutte along the valley to Lermoos and Ehrwald. The line comes in from Füssen in Germany and returns to Germany at Garmisch-Partenkirchen. To get from here to Innsbruck by train one first starts off in the wrong direction, north to Garmisch then via Mittenwald and back into Austria at Scharnitz. Post buses run from Reutte to Innsbruck via Lermoos and Ehrwald.

This area is a popular winter and summer resort. Ehrwald is on the sunny side of the Zugspitze, to quote the town's own claim. It is certainly well equipped, as well as any other in the area. There is a heated indoor swimming pool with sun terrace, and right next door there is a sports hall. To the west of the town, across the footbridge near the tennis courts, are the larch woods and a most lovely walk along gentle gradients, indeed the start is flat.

At the other end of the town is the road up to Obermoos, a footpath goes up through the woods, and the Zugspitze cable car. To get to the summit involves two changes and a most impressive ride. If you are in luck you may spot chamois below. Higher up look out for walkers scrambling up the path from the Wiener-Neustädter Hut. This is a wonderful walk for very experienced hill walkers/scramblers involving 6,500ft of ascent and taking about six hours from Ehrwald. It is an unforgettable experience, if the weather is fair, to climb up and spend the night at the Münchener House, an Alpine hut at the summit, to watch the sunset and then get up early to watch the sunrise. Follow this by the walk back to Ehrwald via the Knorr Hut and the Gatterl.

The view from the top is breathtaking. To the south-east are the High Tauern and the Zillertal Alps. Due south are the Ötztaler Alps with the Silvretta more westerly. North of the Silvretta are the Lechtaler Alps. This forms an unbelievable panorama on a clear day.

There is a border post on the summit and passports may be checked. The westerly summit is in Austria but the highest point, at 2,962 metres (9,716ft) is in Germany. A scramble with fixed ropes and steps permits access to the very summit with its cross.

Many summits have crosses on them, and many of the crosses were erected privately by ordinary citizens as a personal token of gratitude.

An early start is recommended as in high season the tops often get crowded. On the Austrian side there is a restaurant and enclosed viewing area as well as the outside platform. Across the border, in Germany, there is the previously mentioned Münchener House which is an Alpine hut. There is also a restaurant on this side, a cable car down to Eibsee in Germany, and a cable car down to Schneeferner House near the snowfields, where there is good skiing until very late in the year. The Schneeferner House is also the terminus for a railway up from Garmisch-Parten-kirchen.

***

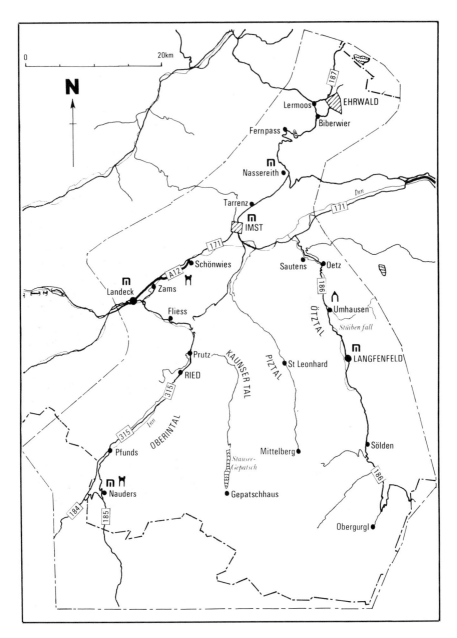

Many people use the terraces for sunbathing but at this altitude great care must be taken. The air is thinner but cooler so tender skin will burn very, very quickly.

Another splendid walk here for very experienced walkers, is as follows. Go down to the lowest level of the Schneeferner House, out onto the terrace and down the steps onto the snow.

Ehrwald village

Follow the snowfield down, following a line of posts to the Knorr Hut which may be reached in one-and-a-half hours. From the hut go right, along level ground at first, to Gatterl, a narrow break in the ridge forming the border, (no formalities) and follow the path right down a narrow chimney with a fixed rope. Go along to another ridge. Go right again, look out for chamois and marmots. At the next ridge the path is obvious; follow it down to the Hochfelder Alm (refreshments) and the Ehrwalder Alm. You may be lucky enough to catch the last cable car down the valley at 5.00pm if the start was early enough. Total walking time is seven hours. There is some rough going, but

25

Lermoos and the Zugspitze

nothing a good hill walker would not enjoy, with fantastic scenery.

For the less ambitious, a trip up the Ehrwald Alm cable car opens up the higher level meadows for a walk without the effort of the climb up. A gentle stroll up to the *Pest Kapelle*, Plague Chapel, is a delight in spring or early summer when the flowers are at their best. The Pest Kapelle was erected by the grateful villagers. At the time when the Black Death was rampant in Europe the villagers were setting off on a pilgrimage. The local militia from the next valley met the pilgrims and prevented them from going on. The plague did not reach the valley and later the chapel was erected in commemoration.

There is a variety of entertainment in the town. A Tyrolean evening can be enjoyed in one of the local hotels, and a host of other entertainments is put on by other establishments.

Moos means moss and the central flat area shows signs of once being peat, but it is now well drained grassland criss-crossed with paths, which make pleasant level walking. Across the Moos is Lermoos, another pleasant resort, the church here is well worth a visit. A chair lift goes up in two stages to the Grubigstein, 2,040 metres, with the possibility of walking down, or at least over the meadows of the lower half.

Biberwier takes up the remaining space in the valley; it is a pleasant little village now that the main road has been diverted. Biberwier's claim to fame is a visible section of the old Roman road, the Via Claudia Augusta, named after Emperior Claudius who rebuilt the road in AD46. Just above the village, off the Fernpass road, there is a summer dry bobsleigh run, or *rodel bahn*. A chair lift whisks passengers up to descend what looks like half a pipe, on a small go-cart-type contraption. No steering is necessary, the only control is a fast/slow device like a joy stick.

The ascent of the Fernpass starts at Biberwier. Take time to stop at the lakes on the way up, Weisensee and Mittersee are splendidly set in woodland with grassy banks and paths round them. The largest lake is the highest one, Blindsee. Delightfully set in a fold of the hills it has a deep green tint that is fully complemented by the forest and the limestone crags above. Road access has made this a popular swimming spot and whole families gather to enjoy a day at the lakeside once the summer sun has warmed the water.

Beyond the lake the summit of the pass is soon reached; at only 1,210

THINGS TO DO ROUND EHRWALD

Ehrwald
Swimming pool, riding, tennis, picturesque village, walks both high and low level, cable car to the Zugspitze, guided walks.

Lermoos
Swimming pool, fishing.

Biberwier
Summer dry bobsleigh run.

Fernpass
Photogenic lakes, lake swimming in Blindsee.

metres it is quite gentle in Alpine terms. There is a large car park just before the summit, and from the terrace of the restaurant there is probably the best view back to the Wetterstein group and the peak of the Sonnenspitze to the north.

Below the summit on the south side Fernstein is soon reached. A castle sits above the road guarding the bridge, below is the lovely Fernsteinsee. The wooded banks of this deep set lake complement the green waters and the tree filled island. Boating and swimming are available and there is a nearby campsite.

Nassereith is the next village, the main square is a stopping place for the Innsbruck to Reutte post bus service. Behind the square is the old part of the village, with some nice old houses and a tiny lake. The village is well known for its carnival procession which is held every five years. These carnivals are held in turn by Nassereith, Imst and Telfs, in February to drive out the bad spirits of winter and prepare for the return of spring. It has its origins in old pagan customs, and the costumed figures wear grotesque masks. When not in use the

Imst

masks are held in Innsbruck in the *Tiroler Volkskunstmuseum,* Tyrol Museum of Popular Art. There is a campsite near the village.

Imst, a few miles beyond Tarrenz, is a thriving market township of almost seven thousand inhabitants, and is an excellent centre to choose for exploration of the surrounding areas. The town lies back from the River Inn and the railway and has two adjacent campsites.

Most attractive is the upper town, or *oberstadt,* which nestles round the old parish church. Destroyed by fire in 1822, it was rebuilt using the original Gothic doorways, and outside there is a giant statue of St. Christopher. Pretty fountains and rounded window grilles make a most attractive sight.

Just across the valley, south, is the Pitztal and there is a bus service from Imst. Some of the figures in the carnival procession are bird sellers. During the seventeenth century canary breeders from Imst traded as far afield as Madrid and St Petersburg. They even had their own depot in London. Their trade began to fall off as competition grew from the popular singing birds from the Harz district. In 1822 there was a disastrous fire in Imst. Many houses were destroyed, including the houses of the canary breeders, and the trade came to an end.

From Imst go south-west on the road No 171. The River Inn soon comes into view, this is crossed to reach the village of Schönwies and recrossed again soon after leaving. There is a campsite at Schönwies. Soon the valley narrows and becomes more wooded. A tiny village, Zamserberg, nestles in the woods below the ruins of Kronburg, a medieval castle.

Within a few kilometres Zams is
reached. From the bridge at Zams there
is a magnificent view of the ruins of
Schrofenstein to the south-west. On
route again it is four kilometres to
Landeck.

Landeck is a small industrial town
with a population of over seven
thousand. It is an important centre,
standing as it does at the junction of the
Inn valley and the Arlberg road. The
massive feudal castle dates from the
thirteenth century. That and the other
strong points perched like eagles' nests
round about silently testify to the
ancient strategic importance of the
valley junction.

Though Landeck lacks the charm of
Imst it still enjoys popularity as a tourist
town. It is a useful centre from which to
explore the nearby Oberinntal and
Kaunertal. It is the main centre and
shopping town for the area. The parish
church is well worth a visit. It stands on
a terrace below the castle. It is a

carefully planned Gothic building and
the fifteenth-century network vaulting is
worth inspecting, as is the centre piece of
the altar. Dating from the sixteenth
century the work represents the
Adoration of the Magi. The side panels
are of later date.

Nearby are Stanz, Tabadill, Fliess and
Grins, all good examples of pretty
Tyrolean villages and are well worth
visiting. Grins was the favourite spa of
the Margravin of Tyrol, Margarete.
Having been widowed and having lost
her son she bequeathed her country to
the Hapsburgs. This was in January,
1363; a few months later she abdicated
and spent the rest of her life in Vienna.

From Landeck take the 315 road
following the river to the higher reaches
of the Inntal. Near the border, just
beyond Pfunds the road divides. The 315
goes over the Reschenpass into Italy and
another branch, now the 184, goes into
Switzerland.

The valley is a paradise for walkers of
all standards, or indeed for anyone
wanting a healthy active holiday. This is
the area for which a claim is made that
the sun shines longer and more brightly
than anywhere else.

Heading upstream the Engadine
valley in Switzerland can soon be
reached via a narrow cleft between
mountains. It is possible to cross into
Switzerland then back to Austria a little
way along at Martina. A short steep
climb on a secondary road brings one
back to Nauders.

A beautiful short walk starts from the
highest point of this road the Norberthöhe. Go west from the Norberthöhe
and in twenty minutes the Schöpfwarte,
at 1,438 metres, is reached. This was
built before World War I, and later
enlarged. There is a most splendid view
from here of the lower Engadine and the
surrounding mountains. A further five

*

Nauders

minutes and another spectacular view is reached, this time of the Inn gorge deep below. Follow the path, marked 2, meandering in a northerly direction before swinging round the Sellesköpfe eventually to return to the starting point. There is another spectacular view, down to the Finstermünz gorge, on the way round. The whole walk is easy going and should be completed in two hours.

Nauders lies in a basin where crops are grown despite the altitude of nearly 1,400 metres. It is mostly a winter sport resort. The castle began life as an administrative centre for the Upper Inn valley. During the Swiss wars of independence it gained in strategic importance. However, the real strategic

THINGS TO DO IN THE UPPER INN VALLEY

Nauders
Walk, viewpoints, old castles, riding, swimming, tennis and fishing.

Pfunds
Picturesque old village, fishing.

Reid im Oberinntal
Nearby villages, cable car in Serfaus and churches.

Feichten
Summer skiing in Kaunertal, freetime centre.

Pontlatzer Bridge
Memorial.

spot on this route is at Finstermünz, or old Finstermünz to be precise. The old road crossed the river at the Innbrücke and a tower was built to straddle the road. This was backed up by a second tower, and natural caves gave more space. Successive enlargements have left nothing earlier than fifteenth century.

From Hochfinstermünz the road clings to the right bank on the cliffs. There is a stopping place on this corniche overlooking the gorge and the tributary gorge leading up to the Swiss Samnaun valley. The main valley is reached at the Kajetanbrücke, and it is two kilometres downstream to Pfunds. There are really two villages, Pfunds-Stuben and Pfunds Dorf, divided by the river Inn.

A corner of Serfaus

Landeck

In the village there are a number of fine old inns and houses which are typical of the area. Express horse-drawn coaches used to run this way to Meron in Italy and to Switzerland, and Pfunds was one of the post stations. In a village of this size there would have been anything up to fifty horses.

Fourteen kilometres down the valley from Pfunds is Ried, from here there is a

St Christoph on the Arlberg

Montafon Valley

Mittersee on the Fernpass

The Gufel Hut

The Upper Reaches of the Kaunertal

side turning to the left up to the interesting villages of Ladis, with its little white bell tower and nearby ruins of Laudeck, and Serfaus. The latter is an important winter sport centre with many ski lifts and, more important to the summer visitor, a cable car going up to a height of 2,000 metres. Ladis, in particular, is well worth a visit to see the old houses with outside staircases and separate baking ovens.

Serfaus has a fourteenth-century and a Baroque church, and some pretty painted houses.

Fendels, by Prutz, is a typical small Tyrolean village in an area of meadows with woods and background of mountains. At Prutz a tributary comes in to join the Inn, and a view opens up

easterly of the Kaunergrat and its jagged skyline. From the head of the deep cut Kaunertal there is a walk along the lake shore to a mountain hut. The road is closed at the Gepatsch, altitude 1,767 metres. Traffic is banned from going higher up the road and it is a pleasant walk along the lake, with splendid mountain views. Allow three hours for the round trip, which is easy going.

The Kaunertal also has summer skiing on Gepatsch glacier, high above the valley floor. A road runs up to the ski lodge and the skiing is between 2,750 and 3,160 metres. This peaceful valley has variety from the glaciers of the mountain tops to the sunbathing on the lawn outside the sport centre, with its indoor pool and bowling alleys.

33

The Pitztal and the Mandarfen

Four kilometres downstream from Prutz, is the Pontlatzer Bridge and a memorial.

In 1342 the earliest of any European democratic constitution was granted to the Tyrol by Meinhard II. All classes were guaranteed their rights. Serfdom was thus unknown in the Tyrol. In 1511 a law was passed granting all Tyroleans the right to bear arms. No one of any class could be called up to serve elsewhere, but all must be ready at all times to defend the Tyrol.

In 1703 the Bavarians and French attacked. Such was the surprise that the authorities in Innsbruck surrendered. The inhabitants of the South Tyrol and the Inn valley forced the invaders to withdraw with heavy losses on the Brenner, at Rattenberg, and here at the Pontlatz Bridge. The memorial also commemorates a defeat in 1809 of a French force marching on Finstermunz.

This historic right and duty of the Tyrolean to bear arms is reflected in the area today. Most villages have a rifle brigade. A feature of many is an open evening when visitors are invited to shoot.

A little further downstream a minor road goes right to Fliess and Piller. There is nothing remarkable about these two small typical villages but they are on route to Wenns and the Pitztal and make a pleasant quiet drive away from the tourist beat. Fliess has a heated swimming pool and facilities for tennis and fishing.

The Pitztal begins at Imst. It ends abruptly after twenty-five miles at Mittelberg and the steely blue shimmering ice wall of a glacier. The several villages along the length of the valley cater for mountain holidays. There are frequent guided walks in the valley and qualified guides are available to accompany rock and ice climbing parties.

Mandarfen, Pitztal

Plangeross, Pitztal ▲

Walkers in the Pitztal

Obergurgl, Ötztal

From the village of Mandarfen, 1,682 metres, there is a chair lift up to a height of 2,298 metres. This is the Riffelsee chair lift, or *Sessellift*. From the top of the chair lift it is an easy climb, of about fifteen minutes, to the summit of the Mutten Kogel, at 2,346 metres. There is a splendid view of the lake and

Obergurgl, Ötztal

surrounding mountains. Near the end of the lake lies the Riffelsee hut with good lake views. The Riffelsee is the largest natural lake in the Ötzaler Alps.

Path No 926 returns to the valley, twisting and turning down to the Taschachalm. From the Alm a road returns to Mandarfen in one-and-a-half kilometres. Total time required is one-and-a-half hours and the going is easy.

To get to the next valley one must go down to the main Inn valley again via Arzl. Five miles downstream another major tributary joins the Inn, the Ötztaler Ache, River. The Ötztal will be remembered for the thundering river and for the shining glaciers. It is a deep valley thirty miles long with ravines separated by more open flatter basins. In 1969 the Timmelsjoch road was completed and the valley ceased to be a dead end. There is now a route, albeit in summer only, south into Italy.

The Ötztaler Alps

Pitztal
Peaceful valley in majestic scenery, mountain walk.

St Leonhard
Two swimming pools, in hotels but open to all. Fishing, guided walks.

Wenns
Leisure centre with indoor tennis, outdoor swimming pool and bowling alley.

ÖTZTAL

Sautens
Swimming pool at the fitness centre.

Ötz
Fishing, woodland walks.

Piburg See
Fishing, bathing, chair lift.

Umhausen
Seventeenth-century inn. Walk to the Stuiben Falls.

Längenfeld
Larch wood walks, Plague Chapel. Heated open-air swimming pool, fishing, riding, tennis, cycle hire, minigolf, museum.

Sölden
Cable car, swimming pool, summer skiing, fishing and riding.

Obergurgl
Chair lift to viewpoint, walks, tennis, two of the hotels have swimming pools.

Hochgurgl
Swimming pool, summer skiing.

Obergurgl stands in a combe at the head of the valley and is the highest village in Austria with a church. In the small square by the church there is a magnificent statue, of an old fashioned mountain guide with outstretched hand pointing to the mountains.

A chair lift goes in two stages to the Hohe Mut, 2,670 metres, where there is a grassy knoll with a mountain restaurant and fantastic views. It is said that twenty-one glaciers can be seen from here. There are certainly snow capped peaks on every side and magnificent waterfalls in the gorges just above the village.

An easy walk to the Rotmoos Water-fall starts from the end of the village road. Follow the path No 922 which goes to the Schönwieshütte. About twenty minutes beyond the bridge over the Gaisberg Bridge turn right to path No 9 to the Rotmoos stream. The stream is magnificent as it hurtles down the ravine. The path back follows path No 7 through the beautiful Zirbenwald and the time for the whole walk should be about two hours, easy going on good paths.

At the nearby village of Hochgurgl, (2,150 metres) there is a heated indoor pool and a chair lift in three stages to a height of over 3,000 metres, where skiing is available all year round.

Down the valley is Sölden, a tourist village popular in both winter and summer. Here there is a cable car which has a spectacular start directly over the main road. It goes up to a height of 3,058 metres to the Geislacherkogel where there are breathtaking views of the entire group of the Ötztal Alps.

Sölden is also the point of departure for one of the highest roads in the Alps, which at its highest point is 2,822 metres. This gives access to winter as well as summer skiing. There is a toll charge for use of the road. Hochsölden is the tourist annexe of the old village; a chair lift operates between the two, joining the higher collection of hotels with the village itself.

The largest village in the valley is Längenfeld, with a population of over three thousand. Nestling in an angle of the valley, the village is really divided into two separate halves by the Fisch-bach which hurls itself down a side valley from the south-east.

There are well prepared walks in the larch woods near the village. On the west side of the valley is a seventeenth-century *Pest Kappelle,* or plague chapel, one of the more charming views among

Sölden, Ötztal

the harder scenery of the peaks which seem to close in all round.

Even at this height, (Längenfeld is 1,180 metres) crops are grown. Indeed they are grown even higher up the valley. The reason is that the upper end of the Ötztal has a channel between the peaks through which a current of warm southerly air finds its way. This current keeps the valleys warm and dry and allows even barley, for example, to be grown at a height of 1,700 metres.

While Längenfeld is the largest village in the valley Umhausen is the oldest. A large inn, the Gasthaus Krone, is typical of the district. Customers of the inn may see a room still furnished in seventeenth-century style. From the tourist office a signposted track leads to the Stuiben-fälle, a picturesque cascade where the torrent tumbles down the rocky ravine. At a chalet-restaurant cross the stream and walk up the left bank. About two hours are required for the walk.

Ötz is the last village on the return trip down the valley. The large village church is built on a level spot on the sunny slope.

Timmels Pass, Ötztal

The warm southerly air current, or Föhn,which blows down the valley can transform life. The Föhn, at its worst, can be used as extenuating circumstances in criminal trials. Examinations may be suspended in schools. Föhn headaches are infamous. This warm air which allows crops to be grown higher up the valley also allows peach and apricot orchards to thrive in the Ötz basin.

Near Ötz is the hamlet of Piburg and the Piburger See, at 915 metres. This jewel of a lake has a fascinating history. In 1282 it was given to Stams Monastery, which had then just been founded.

Until 1500 meat was forbidden to the monks so the fish yield of the lake was important. The rights of the monks to the lake were reaffirmed in 1339 by Duke Johann and again in 1616 by Archduke Max. For six hundred years the lake remained as a holding of the monastery. The tenants at nearby Piburg were forbidden to fish. A story is told that in the middle of the nineteenth century bathers caused frequent annoyance and the monastery sold the lake.

It was sometime round about the end of the century when the first bathing hut was built, for the convenience of hotel guests from Ötz. In 1929 the lake and surroundings were declared a nature conservation area. The first limnological studies were carried out in 1931; they are now confined to a bay at the northern end so that they do not intrude into the landscape. The Piburger See remains one of the few completely natural unspoilt lakes anywhere in Europe despite its use as an amenity. This use has been very carefully controlled. Summer 1982 saw a new bathing establishment, built on concrete pillars and anchored to the bank to avoid felling many trees.

There is a parking area near the beginning of Piburg and there are lakeside walks in magnificent unspoilt scenery. The lake temperature can get as high as 24°C in summer, making it quite comfortable and one of the warmest lakes in the Tyrol.

Below Ötz the main road along the Inn valley is reached once more. Turn eastwards along the 171 towards Innsbruck.

*

3 Around Innsbruck

The first place of any significance on the road to Innsburck is Stams, where Stams Monastery is very well worth visiting. Its history is as follows:

Conradin Hohenstaufen was the last of his line; his father was dead and his mother, Elizabeth of Bavaria, subsequently married Meinhard II, Count of Görz and Tyrol. Conradin was beheaded in Naples on the order of Charles of Anjou, in 1268. His mother Elizabeth founded the monastery to his memory, though she did not live to see its consecration. The monastery rapidly gained in influence, and until 1600 all sovereign princes of the Tyrol were buried at Stams.

This majestic Baroque building was made more conspicuous in the seventeenth century by the addition of two towers. There is room to park in the esplanade near the fourteenth-century village church, and the entrance is through the abbey gateway to the porter's lodge of the monastery. Altered many times, the present Baroque style is the result of the last rebuilding in the eighteenth century. The showpiece of the Abbey church furnishings is the high altar with its representation of the Tree of Life. The form of the branches of the tree are eighty-four carved figures representing Saints surrounding the Virgin. On either side Adam and Eve represent life's beginning, at the top Christ on the cross represents the mystery of the supernatural.

The Hall of Princes is reached by a staircase with a fine wrought iron balustrade going up from the porter's lodge. In the Hall of State paintings depict many episodes in the life of St Bernard. A guided tour and an English language brochure are available.

Telfs, only seven kilometres from Stams, is a typical market town. It was the limit of navigation of the Inn and even then could only be used by smaller boats. Here everything had to be unloaded for transport overland up the Fernpass or up to the Arlberg or Engadine.

The masked dances and carnivals of Telfs (see Chapter 3) are prehistoric in origin. They will probably never die, although perhaps the reason for them has altered, for the Tyrolean love of pageant and play-acting will ensure their survival even if the tourist industry does not.

From Telfs there is a minor road towards Mösern and Seefeld in Tyrol. The splendid site of the village of Mösern is an ideal place for a stop. On the way up to the village there are splendid retrospective views, towards the north-west, of the Mieminger Mountains. In Mösern on a grassy spur below the church is the Gasthof Inntal, from where there is a splendid view of the River Inn, upstream in the Telfs furrow, before it disappears from view in the tangle of peaks, some covered with snow.

Seefeld in Tyrol is five kilometres away; an elegant place with a high reputation as a ski resort due to the fact that the Olympics were held here twice. The parish church is worth visiting, a Gothic building dating from the fifteenth century. There are interesting murals in the chancel, of the same date,

Cable car to the Seefelder Joch

which have been restored. This picturesque town is a winter and summer
resort. It is one of the few places to boast
a full size golf course. Facilities for
riding are nearby and there is a casino.
The splendid sport centre has indoor
and outdoor pools, there are twelve
outdoor and four indoor tennis courts.

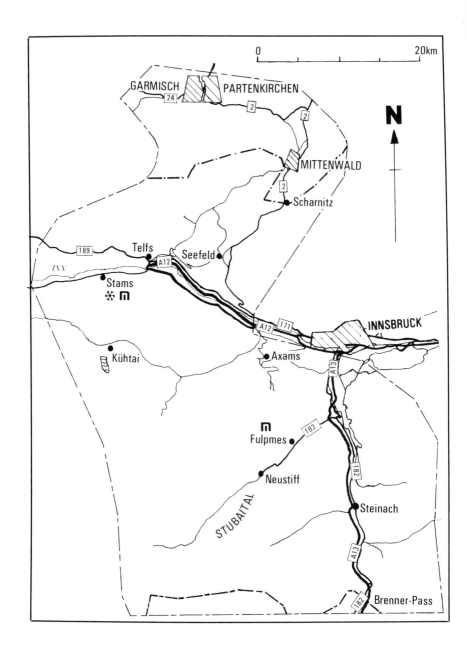

Rowing, fishing, bowling and mini golf are all available, and many of the hotels have their own pools, and saunas.

A minor road leaves Seefeld towards Leutasch. The road leads through a wooded landscape towards the charming unspoilt Leutasch valley. Leutasch itself is an attractive jumble of hamlets; the valley is flat and broad. The covered heated swimming pool has a cafe

restaurant attached and also a large outside sunbathing lawn. A climbing school, a riding school and two chair lifts complete the facilities. One chair lift to the south takes one to a height of 1,600 metres, from the hamlet of Moos to the Moos Alm, on the eastern end of the ridge of the Hohe Munde (2,592 metres). A good path climbs from the alm to the summit.

The valley lies at the east foot of the Wetterstein Mountains, with the Karwendels to the east and Miemingers to the south-west. To return drive north-east towards Mittenwald in Germany, where the border checks are minimal, but on the outskirts of the town turn back south to recross the border to Scharnitz.

The drive towards Mittenwald with the roofed roadside crosses, houses with large stones on their roofs, to keep them on in winter gales, enables one to enjoy the primitive air of a high alpine valley.

Scharnitz is a pleasant, small border village with bus and rail links. It is mostly passed through by people rushing south to Innsbruck or over the Brenner Pass to Italy. However, it is a convenient place from which to explore the Isar valley or the Karwendel Mountains.

There are easy footpaths each side of the Karwendel group. East of the village, crossing the railway, the Pürzlweg climbs steeply to the Pürzl *Kapelle,* or chapel, then follows the Karwendel valley, which is surprisingly level, to the Larchetalm on a good forest road. The Larchetalm is privately owned, but higher up the valley the Karwendelhaus may be found. This is an alpine hut and clings to a rocky perch almost at the saddle before the descent to the Johannestal.

This is a good walk; two hours to the

Larchetalm and two more to the Karwendelhaus, and then the return. The valley is beautiful; entirely unspoilt, closed to traffic except for forestry, farmers and the Larchetalm and Karwendelhaus vehicles, it is delightful. There are great towering mountains on both sides but pleasant green meadows and woods on the lower slopes. The Karwendel *Bach,* or stream, tumbles gaily down joined by side streams at many places.

There is a second walk which follows the River Isar upstream on a small road at first, but before the Scharnitzer Alm is reached, the road is closed to traffic and follows the river. One mile beyond the Wiesenhof, take a right fork which soon crosses the river. The next right fork leads to a path by which one can return on the south bank.

The next village is Reith by Seefeld.

The village church is in a charming setting and worth visiting. Reith is at 1,130 metres and the road plunges down into the Inn valley, passing the hamlet of Leithen. The well known slope down to the valley is called the Zirler Berg. There is a descent of 500 metres in just over four kilometres. At one time, so it is said, spectators used to collect near the hairpin bends to watch for accidents. Before improvements, the road was as steep as 1 in 4, but now it is 1 in 7 and only one hairpin bend remains. There is now a car park and cafe, and a splendid viewpoint over the Rosskogel to the Kalkkögel ridge to the south.

The valley carries the motorway and the main road to Innsbruck, but due south is another of the charming unspoilt valleys so typical of the Tyrol, the Sellrain. This is easily reached from Innsbruck by bus, and is very popular

The Karwendel House,
deep in the mountains

Kühtai Hotel

with locals from Innsbruck as a winter sport area. In summer the valley villages are starting points for tours of the Stubai glaciers.

Kühtai stands at the head of the valley, (1,966 metres) on a plateau, with the renowned hunting lodge of Maxmilian I, now converted to a hotel. Beyond the pass, at 2,017 metres, the road goes down to Ötz (Chapter 3). There is a minor road to the south just beyond the pass. A little way down this road, there is a footpath which forks to the left. It soon forks right to the

*

Kühtai

Axamer Lizum in winter

Finstertaler Speicher, one of the larger lakes, formed by a dam. The path No 146 starts from the Hotelsiedlung Kühtai, and is easy going, taking about one-and three-quarter-hours. There are splendid views and the many small lakes in the area ornament the landscape like jewels.

Coming back down the valley the villages of St Sigmund, and Gries in Sellrain may be found, where there is a side valley south to the hamlets of Praxmar and Lüsens. This is an ideal place to get away from the crowds and enjoy the real Tyrol. The next village is Sellrain and at the bottom of the valley, Kematen.

On emerging from the Sellrain valley there is a right turn on a minor road to Völs. There is a further right turn to Götzens through the village to Axams then up to Axamer-Lizum, at 1,564 metres. This is well worth a visit. It was the site of the 1964 Winter Olympics. There is a funicular, Olympia Standseilbahn, which will carry passengers to the mountain station restaurant at 2,340 metres. A little downhill, to the Hoadl Sattel, (2,264 metres) leads one to a grassy plateau which is rich in all kinds of alpine flowers. The paths are good and safe for a gentle stroll in the most beautiful mountain scenery.

Axams is a splendid old village with modern facilities for tourists; the swim-

Axams

Stams
Monastery.

Telfs
Bus and rail stations. Indoor and outdoor swimming pools.

Seefeld in Tyrol
Boating, golf (eighteen hole), bowling, fishing, walking, riding, tennis, indoor and outdoor swimming pools, minigolf, casino.

Leutasch
Riding, swimming, fishing, chair lifts.

Scharnitz
Small border town. Centre for walking in the Isar valley and Karwendel Mountains.

Reith
Nearby viewpoint on the road below the pretty village.

Sellrain
Beautiful unspoilt valley rising to 2,017 metres.

Kühtai
At the summit of the Sellrain valley, high level easy walk.

ming pool is delightful. There is a walking programme and facilities for cycle hire, with a cycle track laid out specially through the meadows. There are the usual musical events, band concerts, Tyrolean evenings and church concerts. Tennis, minigolf and bowling are included in the attractions of this lovely centre, which is only nine kilometres from Innsbruck.

Nearby Mutters is a farming village which has kept its country air despite catering for tourists. It lies on moderately level ground. There is a four-person cable car to the Mutter alm, a twenty-minute ride to a splendid walking area. Near the village is a splendid heated open-air pool, (or pools, as there are really four if one counts the paddling pools). These are surrounded by grassy banks for sunbathing. Close by are the tennis courts. Scattered about the area are a number of camp sites. Leaving Mutters, the road soon joins the main road No 182. Innsbruck is only two or three kilometres away to the north. The Wipptal is south with its side valleys. The main valley carries the motorway over the Brenner Pass. This has been a favourite route since the very earliest recorded history. It is the shortest route from Germany to Italy and was maintained and kept open, even in winter (which was no mean feat) by the Romans. The Wipptal is spanned by the famous Europa Bridge, which carries the motorway up to the Brenner and into the South Tyrol, which is in Italy.

There are four side valleys, the most famous of which is the Stubaital which offers splendid opportunities for mountain climbing. As an excellent excursion from Innsbruck, there is the narrow gauge 'Stubai Valley Railway'. This runs exclusively to the Stubai valley and terminates at Fulpmes. Post buses run at frequent intervals from Innsbruck to Ranalt.

The road continues past Ranalt to the Mutterberg Alm where the cable cars start for the glacier. The journey is in two parts, with a break at the Dresdener Hut, (2,308 metres) and a change to the next stage which goes up to 2,900 metres. Here there is all-year-round skiing, walking on good safe paths, and for the skiers a double chair lift and seven tow lifts. Unless one intends to ski there is little point in using the top section of the cable car; instead, take a stroll from the Dresdener Hut. There are paths to the Trögler (2,901 metres) to the

Europa Bridge in winter

east, or to the Egesengrat (2,631 metres) west then north-east.

Ranalt is more or less a collection of farms at the foot of glaciers; Volderau and Milders are hamlets offering peaceful stopping places in this delightful setting. Neustift is another of those delightful villages that has everything to offer the visitor. Sixty kilometres of pathways are looked after by the local council who ensure that they are tidy, safe and secure for visitors, and that the signposting is adequate. There are two heated swimming pools, indoor and

outdoor. The outdoor pool has a sunbathing lawn. Tennis can be played either on one of the nine outdoor or two indoor courts. Fishing and riding are also available here, as are the usual evening entertainments.

At Fulpmes, where the railway ends, there is a tennis hall with a sliding roof which can be opened in warm weather. There is also a heated pool. The village is beautifully situated in broad green meadows below the forested approaches to the higher peaks. There is a camp site higher up the valley, and at the lower end there are three more. The train will take you back to Innsbruck, after first climbing to the high plateau at the entrance to the valley, then going by way of Telfs, Mutters and Natters.

Schönberg stands at the junction of the main valley and the Stubai valley. The Wipptal is not one of the most beautiful valleys in the Tyrol; however, it is popular with the Austrians as a winter and summer resort area. Up the valley first stop is Matrei. The village was rebuilt in typical Tyrolean style after being almost completely destroyed during World War II, and the houses blend well with the surroundings. Many of the houses have painted murals on the outside walls which are very attractive.

The next village is Steinach, where there is a lake and a swimming pool. Here also there is a road branching off into the Gschnitztal. Two hamlets decorate this short romantic valley. Trims is not quite halfway up the valley; Gschnitz is to be found at the head, at an altitude of 1,242 metres. Beyond Steinach the road climbs to Gries, which is not far from the head of the pass. Nearby there is a reminder that this was once a military road of Imperial Rome, and there are some interesting remains. Quite soon after leaving the ruins the top of the pass is reached.

Between Steinanch and Gries there is a minor road giving direct access, via the hamlet of Vinaders, to the Obernberger-tal where the hamlet of Obernberg am Brenner is strung out along the upper reaches of the valley. Beyond the guest house Waldesruh, where there is a large car park, the road is private and closed to traffic but continues up to the Obernberger See, at 1,590 metres. It is a three-quarters-of-an-hour walk up the road to the lake where there are good views. Nearby but slightly higher there is the Seekappelle, or lake chapel, which

was built on its little hill in 1935. The path goes right round the lake and also continues south to the Portjoch, a pass on the Italian border. From here are extensive views of the peaks of the Dolomites and, just below, the Pflerschtal.

The walk to the pass, which goes up to 1,836 metres, takes approximately four-and-a-half hours, and to the lake two-and-a-half. On the lower parts and round the lake there is a mixture of larchwoods and alpine meadows. The paths are moderate and well marked.

From just below Gries there is yet another valley, this time going east, which divides at the hamlet of St Jodock, where the tourist office is to be found. The southern spur goes to Vals

---

THINGS TO DO SOUTH OF INNSBRUCK

Axams
The Axamer-Lizum funicular, swimming, cycling, tennis and walking.

Mutters
Swimming, cable car and tennis.

Stubaital
All year skiing. High level walks.

Neustift
Swimming, fishing, tennis, riding and walks.

Fulpmes
Swimming, fishing and tennis.

Obernberg
Lakeside walk, 1,590 metres

Side valleys
Peaceful quiet valleys in superb scenery.

The main valley has rail and bus links, most of the side valleys have post bus services.

and the northern branch goes to Schmirn and Kasern. From Matrei there is a valley east to the village of Navis.

All these side valleys are well off the tourist track though they do cater for tourists, and nearly all have information offices so that one can find those delightful evening events that are so much a part of the Tyrolean scene. There are picturesque hamlets and pretty little churches and chapels all set against a backdrop of pinewoods and snowcapped mountains.

Not to be missed, even if the climb up the Brenner is not attempted, is the Ellbögen Road. Once this was a road used for the transport of salt and runs between Matres and the main Inn valley. It is east and on the other side of the river Sill from the high road and the motorway. Passing the villages of Gedeier, where there is a campsite, and

Mühlthal, the village of Patsch is soon reached. On the southern outskirts of Patsch there is a splendid view south-west along the length of the Stubaital. There is a road to Igls from here.

Igls is a resort made more popular since the 1976 Winter Olympic Games. There are facilities for fishing, there is a nine hole golf course and the sports facilities reflect the nearness of Innsbruck. The city can be reached quickly by the frequent buses or by trams which also run out to Igls. The village has an indoor swimming pool, but in summer months a favourite spot is the Lanser See, a small bathing lake. It lies a kilometre from Igls on the edge of the plateau, while Igls itself lies back at the foot of the mountain. However, the real lure is the cable car to the Patscher-kofel. The valley station is at 903 metres. There is an intermediate station called

Igls

Heiligwasser, Holy Water, where the spring water is said to be a panacea for all ills. This used to be very popular as a place of pilgrimage. The summit station of the cable car lies at 1,952 metres, and there is a hotel and restaurant where refreshments may be obtained. A chair lift continues on to the very summit at 2,246 metres; this is above the tree line of course and there are spectacular views. North is Innsbruck and beyond the Karwendel range, north-west is the Miemingers and north of them the Zugspitze in the Wetterstein group marking the border with Germany. To the north-east beyond the Karwendel group the valley up to Achensee can be spotted and beyond is the Rofan group. Countless glaciers can be seen to the south-west in the Stubaier Alps while south-east the near mountains are the Tuxer Alps; the peaks beyond are the Zillertal Alps.

On the top there are many safe paths for an afternoon stroll, taking in the views. A good walk may be made by first taking the cable car to the summit station. Path 32 leads to the Bascheben (a snack bar) Jausen-station, on the Zirbenweg. There is a ridge path east then north, still on the Zirbenweg, and in the direction of the Viggarspitze. Path No 48 forks left, north-east, off the Zirbenweg. The path then goes down via Isshütte to the Sistranser Alm, where refreshments are available. Path No 49 leads to the Lanser Alm and path No 4 to the Igler Alm and on to Heiligwasser where the cable car can be taken down again. The time for the walk is approximately three hours, easy going. The Igler Alm is a guest house and there is also a guest house at Heiligwasser.

The use of the word Alm is often misleading. It means Alp or alpine pasture, and is dotted about on detailed maps quite frequently. Often there is a farmhouse or building site, and quite often modern practice has turned the farmhouse into a guest house. At the simpler, more remote Alms the fare is simple too; bread and cheese and beer for example. Often an Alm will be a much grander affair much more like a restaurant, especially where the tourist demand is being catered for.

4 Innsbruck

Innsbruck, (bridge over the Inn) received its charter in 1239. It is the capital and cultural centre of the Tyrol, and is reputed to be one of the most beautiful towns of its size in the world. The old part of the town is a pedestrian precinct from 10.30am, allowing the visitor to appreciate the beauties without the attendant risks and annoyance from cars.

Innsbruck is young by camparison with Wilten. This contained the oldest monastic house in the North Tyrol. The legend has it that in the sixth century the giant Raymon killed his rival Thyrsus near Seefeld. He was overcome by

Old houses on the river bank, Innsbruck

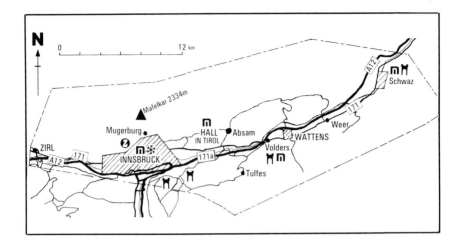

remorse and, having long admired the Benedictines of Tegernsee, he decided to build a monastery. Using blocks of limestone left by the Romans at their old town of *Veldidena* (Wilten), he proceeded to build. The work was sorely hampered by a dragon which playfully pulled down the stones by wrapping its tail around them. The workmen begged Raymon to deal with the fearsome monster. According to legend Raymon chased the dragon into a cave and killed it in masterly fashion. So began what is now a suburb of Innsbruck. Innsbruck itself began in 1180 when Count Berthold of Andechs bartered with Wilten Abbey for the land on which now stands the old centre of Innsbruck. The existing village was developed into a market town. Possibly a chalice and paten were part of the price he had to pay. They are two of what were Wilten's greatest treasures, and are now in a museum in Vienna.

Innsbruck in the twelfth century was an important trading post. The fact that it commanded one of the most important trade routes across the Alps is no doubt part of this success. Boats travelled up the Inn to Hall in Tyrol before unloading. This is only a few miles downstream from Innsbruck and many of the goods travelled up to the Arlberg or up to the Oberinntal and into the Swiss Engadine. Traffic from Germany came this way over the Scharnitz and Brenner passes.

Innsbruck's prosperity increased when, in the early fifteenth century, Duke Friedrich transferred his official residence from Meran. Thus Innsbruck became the official capital of the Tyrol.

The city also benefited in the reign of Maria Theresa. At the southern end of Maria Theresa Strasse stands the Triumphal Arch. In 1767 the imperial family were celebrating the marriage of Leopold, Grand Duke of Tuscany, to Maria Ludovica, the Infanta of Spain. The Emperor Franz, husband of Maria Theresa, died suddenly during the celebrations. That is the reason why on the southern face of the arch the sculptured reliefs commemorate the marriage, while those on the northern face commemorate the funeral trappings.

North from the Triumphal Arch, there is one of the most famous views in Europe which can be seen from half way up the street. It is best viewed from the left-hand side. This is the Nordkette, the chain of the peaks of the Karwendel range.

The column in the centre of the street is St Anne's Column, *Annasäule;* this commemorates 26 July 1703, when an invading force of Bavarians retreated during the War of the Spanish Succession. Place of honour on top of the column is given to The Virgin. Round the base are the figures of Saints Anne (on whose birthday the retreat occurred), George, Vigilus and Cassianus.

Straight ahead is Herzog Friedrich Strasse, a busy street with arcades of shops. At the end is the Little Golden Roof, *Goldenes Dachl.*

This charming and unique balcony

The Golden Roof, view from the town tower, Innsbruck

which was finished in 1500, with its golden roof, was built on the instructions of Maximilian I as a place of comfort and a vantage point from which dancing in the square below could be viewed. A tradition existed for centuries that the structure was built by Archduke Friedrich, nicknamed Friedrich the Penniless, Duke of Tyrol 1406-1439, to put to an end the jokes about his poverty. The balcony juts out on a corner. Almost on the opposite corner is the Stadtturm. This belfry stands alongside the old town hall. The octagonal renaissance structure rises from a square base. It bristles with turrets and is surmounted with a dome and lantern. The tower is open from April to September between 9.00am and 5.00pm and an English language brochure is available.

Look towards the Golden Roof and on the left corner is the Helblinghaus. In the eighteenth century this was given a Rococo facing with lavishly decorated window frames. The bow windows are a style often seen in southern Germany. a remedy for the darkness of narrow city streets.

A little further on, on the left, is the famous old inn *Goldener Adler,* Golden Eagle. In proud memory of the famous guests it has received since the sixteenth century there is a marble plaque outside with their names carved on it. On the same street, the Hofburg can also be found. The building was erected piece-meal by the Hapsburgs. Maria Theresa had the present palace built; her husband died here during the marriage festivities of their daughter in 1765. The two towers flanking the Palace were finished in 1770 and the building is a good example of Baroque civil architecture in Innsbruck. Of particular interest in the state rooms, which are open to the public, is the *Riesensaal,*

The Hofburg, Innsbruck

Giants' Hall. This state room, 31 metres long, is lined with stucco panels and the ceiling was painted in 1776 by Franz Anton Maulpertsch. The triumph of the House of Hapsburg is the theme and is typified by two women holding out their hands to each other. Paintings on the walls are of Maria Theresa's children and other relatives and descendants, including Louis XVI and Marie Antoinette.

To the rear of the Hofburg is the Cathedral of St James, *Dom zu St Jakob,* which was rebuilt in the early eighteenth century. The old town surrounds the cathedral, making a most colourful picture with ancient balconied houses. The Hofburg is open 9.00am to 4.00pm with guided tours, in English, taking about thirty-five minutes. The cathedral is open 6.00am to noon and 2-5pm, but is closed on Fridays, Sundays and holiday mornings.

Across the road from the Hofburg is the Imperial Chapel. The nave and three aisles are of equal size, built to contain Maximilian's mausoleum. The building is in Gothic style, though the tower and entrance porch are Renaissance, and there are Baroque additions. On the gallery there are twenty-three statues of the protecting saints of the Hapsburg family; they are more graceful than the colossi guarding the tomb.

The Hofgarten offers the chance to rest and relax near the Hofburg. There are shady walks, weeping willows and lakes in this beautiful garden, and in the summer months there are evening concerts.

Innsbruck has three main museums. First there is the *Tiroler Volkskunst Museum,* Tyrol Museum of Popular Art, open from 9.00am to 5.00pm and to

Bronze figures in the Hofkirche on the tomb of Kaiser Maximilian I, Innsbruck

Fifteenth-century statue of the Christ child from the Volkskunstmuseum, Innsbruck

noon on Sundays and holidays, with an English language brochure available.

Here there are examples of animal stalls, fine rooms with panelling and stoves from peasants houses. On the first floor is a collection of models of Tyrolean houses, stone buildings from the Upper Inn Valley and wooden ones from Zillertal. Also included are domestic utensils, games, tools and musical instruments. There are large collections of furniture and peasant costumes including the ones used at the Imst carnival. Textiles and looms, glass and pottery are also on display giving a picture of what life was like in the region in bygone times.

The Tiroler Landeskundliches Museum is devoted to the development of fine arts in the Tyrol, with many paintings, woodwork and minerals, and a section devoted to the history of the closely connected with the origins of Innsbruck. The Abbey Church can be recognized by the red roughcast. It dates from the seventeenth century, but it was restored in 1944 after it had been damaged. Two stone giants guard the doorway; the narthex is enclosed by a magnificent grille dating from 1707 and contains another statue representing a giant, this time in wood and reputed to be Raymon, who founded the Abbey. The series of altar pieces, the paintings and the work above the high altar are all worthy of closer inspection.

Almost across the road is Wilten Basilica. The monastery had the parish church of Wilten completely restored between 1751 and 1756 in order to perpetuate the devotions to Our Lady of the Four Columns, who had been the object of pilgrimage to Innsbruck since the Middle Ages. In 1957 the church was raised to the status of Basilica. Inside there are a great many works by the artists of the Rococo period. At the high altar is the statue of The Virgin which was the object of the pilgrimages.

South of the motorway, which is close by, is Bergisel. This was the scene of a battle in 1809 when the hero of the Tyrol Andreas Hofer, defeated the French invaders. On the wooded hill there are

Tyrol and another to mountain buildings.

The third museum is the Kaiserjägermuseum, Memorial to the Imperial Light Infantry. The musem traces the history of the corps and contains mementoes of the 1809 uprising. On the ground floor there is a memorial of World War I. There are celebrated uniforms, arms and paintings of this celebrated Tyrolean corps which was disbanded in 1919. Many of the windows give good views of the town and of the mountains of the Nordkette.

In the old part of the town, Wilten, there are some places of historic interest, well worth visiting. There is Wilten Abbey Church or *Stiftkirche,* which is

Karwendel mountains from near Schwaz

several monuments by the pleasantly laid-out walks, including of course one to Andreas Hofer. After the War of Liberation in 1809 the hill became a rifle range, which was used by the Kaiserjäger. At the end of the century it

Castle Ambras, Innsbruck

became a Field of Remembrance. The monuments not to be missed include the Provincal Cenotaph and the Tomb of the Unknown Soldier. There is also a small lookout tower. Widely spread monuments amid beautiful woods and lawns are the great charm of Bergisel, and the place is a favourite among the locals in search of peace and relaxation. In the background is the ski jump built for the 1964 Olympic Games.

On the opposite side of the city is the Bergisel Panorama, *Riesenrundgemälde*. This huge circular fresco was done in honour of Andreas Hofer and depicts the Battle of Bergisel.

Near the memorial is one of Innsbruck's favourite outings, to the Hungerberg, which can be reached from Innsbruck by a cog railway from the town. Here the valley station of the Hafelekar cable car is situated. The summit is 2,334 metres high and is reached in two stages, on the north wall. The city lies at the foot directly below, and to the south there are the southern ranges with glaciers as far as the eye can see. To the north are the Karwendel Mountains with the highest point the Birkkarspitz at 2,756 metres. There are safe, well-defined footpaths to stroll along admiring the views, and mountain hotels for refreshments. Cars leave at least hourly from 8.15am in the summer season.

Another outing from Innsbruck is Ambras Castle, which is open daily, except Tuesdays, from May to October. Buses run from Innsbruck to the village of Ambras half-hourly for the half-hour trip. This magnificent castle is one of the best-preserved in Austria. There was a castle on the site built by the Dukes of Andechs in the eleventh century.

However, Archduke Ferdinand had the place completely rebuilt. In 1576 the family moved in but building went on for about twenty years. The Spanish Hall was built in 1570, the earliest known large Renaissance hall in the German speaking countries.

One thing invariably remains in the memory of visitors: Phillippine Wetser's bath. Phillippine and Archduke Ferdinand the Second married in secret in 1557. The poor lady lived under a cloud, though she was said to be happy. A marriage without parental permission, under imperial law, was invalid. However, Ferdinand's father, Emperor Ferdinand I, forgave the couple when Phillippine begged forgiveness, but as she was a commoner he insisted that the marriage should remain secret. This meant that though she was the Archduke's legal wife, the world did not know and thought she was his mistress. Even after she was dead there was mystery. The rumour spread, as late as 1705, that she had been murdered in her giant bath. In 1889 an eminent historian complained to the Austrian Historical Society that visitors to the castle were being told of the murder. In truth Phillippine had died in bed, while her husband was with her. Her memory is still revered by the people of Innsbruck. Her magnificent bath was copper lined, measured six feet by nine and took one hundred and eighty gallons of water.

The castle is almost two groups of buildings, the lower castle including the entrance lodge and the upper castle which is where the former medieval fortress stood. A great part of the Archduke's personal collection has been transferred, long ago, to Vienna. However, there is still an impressive display of weapons and armour along with equipment used in jousting. This is in the lower castle. On the way to the upper castle is the Spanish Room with its Renaissance inlaid ceiling. There is a room (the Kunst und Wunderkammer) which houses a collection of rare objects ranging from animal to mineral. Other exhibits are household gadgets and curiosities dating from medieval times.

The grounds of the castle are attractively laid out and are extensive, they contain the original jousting area and deep in the woods is a small cemetry where lie heroes of the War of Liberation.

Five guided tours a day, the first at 10.00am, take one-and-a-quarter hours each, so with a tour of the grounds and lunch this alone is a day's outing, and well worth the time spent.

Another pleasant short outing from Innsbruck is the Ehnbach-Klamm which is near Zirl. Here, through a wild gorge, a pathway has been carved through the rocks making a fine attraction.

The Alpine Zoo is another attraction of interest to children and adults alike. It is open all year every day from 9am, and can be reached by bus from the Maria Theresa Strasse, or by a comfortable half-hour walk. Here all alpine animals and birds can be seen: marmot, beaver, vulture, eagle, eagle-owl, lizards and snakes and many more. The mountain walker may by fortunate, if out early enough and walking quietly, to see chamois quite close or even see an eagle soaring. After rain lizards come out on the quiet paths high up. But this collection of birds and animals can be viewed closely. Animals not often seen in zoos, the marmot for example or the chamois, make this opportunity a must.

To complete the attractions of Innsbruck there is an indoor swimming pool, facilities for riding and an eighteen-hole golf course.

The road east from Innsbruck leads to Hall in Tyrol which is only seven

Hall in Tyrol

kilometres away. An observant citizen once noticed a deer licking a rock near Hall. This was in 1280, and subsequently the Hall salt industry began. At one time the population of Hall was larger than that of Innsbruck, but the choice of the the latter as the centre of government, and imperial residence, settled the matter and Hall ceased to expand.

No one quite knows why this medieval town grew up so close to Innsbruck. Was it because this was where the river became navigable? There is just as much water at Innsbruck, and Innsbruck was where the first bridge was built. However, Hall became the place where the great river boats stopped and unloaded. Up to twenty horses drew these boats, which often had smaller craft in tow. The journey upstream from Kufstein took five days, but the return journey took only six hours. Only small craft

went up, past Innsbruck to Telfs. Goods also came upstream on log rafts and when the goods were unloaded the rafts were dismantled and used for firewood to stoke the boilers of the salt industry.

The old mint in Hall was founded in 1477. Rich finds of silver had been made in the mines at Schwaz, thirty kilometres east along the valley, and this made the journey to the old mint at Meran inconvenient. Added reasons were distrust of the Swiss, and Turkish incursions to the south, both of which might have designs on the old mint.

Austrian patriots like to point out that the word 'dollar' originated from the Taler which took its name from the Inntal.

Hall in Tyrol has a splendid medieval 'old town'. The Unterer Stadtplatz is an open space formed by the main road; the main place of interest is the beautiful

On the Grubigstein, above Lermoos

Lermoos and the Zugspitze

Oberer Stadtplatz. This is not a square but an irregular space bounded by several picturesque and interesting buildings. Radiating from the square are several beautiful streets.

The *Rathaus,* or town hall, is the building with the high roof. The main part of the building is sixteenth century and carries some delicately carved designs, and the statue of a knight with the coat of arms of Austria and the Tyrol.

The parish church, *Statdpfarrkirche,* dates from the fifteenth century and is surrounded by additions and annexes including the chapel of St Jospeh, and one dedicated to the Knight Florian Waldauf. Along with the Herz Jesus Basilica this is well worth visiting.

The best time to visit is on a Saturday, when the Oberer Stadtplatz is closed to traffic. Leave by way of the Rosengasse which leads towards the Stiftsplatz. Here, buildings are in a classical arrangement, in contrast to the old town. They form a square, and were formerly a convent and a church and college of Jesuits. Nearby is the *Damestift,* Ladies Abbey, which was founded in 1567 by Archduchess Magdalene, who is remembered by a statue in the square.

Forming a half circle to the north and west are magnificent boulevards known as the Stadtgraben, which helps make this small town so attractive.

There is a museum in the town, the Museum Old Hall, which houses exhibits of old life styles and houses, and

The Old Mint, Hall in Tyrol

Town view, Hall in Tyrol

also of the salt workings. Between the river and the Unterer Stadtplatz is Münzergasse, where the lovely old tower, the Münzerturm, may be found. There is an open air swimming pool and a campsite nearby.

This jewel of a town, set between the river and the mountains, is surrounded by meadows and there are some small villages nearby to explore. From Tulfes, to the south, is a cable car ascending to 2,000 metres and offering splendid views of this wider part of the valley.

An interesting and gentle stroll from Hall in Tyrol is to take any of the side roads north to Absam, then to go by way of the guest house Walder Brücke and on to the Walder Kapelle. From here the Egholungsweg goes through the woods to St Martin, where there is an interesting church. The Waldlepfad leads on in the same direction to the next hamlet, St Michael. There is a south turn to Fritzens, which soon joins a road but there is a right turn, westerly, to follow a track just south of the woods to Baumkirchen, where another track just south of the woods leads to Grüneck and back to Hall. The route is about ten miles, or just over sixteen kilometres. There is an ascent of about 300 metres and the route is well served with places of refreshment.

Another interesting walk from Hall is to follow Lendgasse from the Unterer Stadtplatz, cross the railway and follow the road to where it recrosses. Do not cross the railway again but take the path near the river, downstream. Cross the river by the road bridge, returning the same way. The round trip is six kilometres, or three-and-a-half miles, mostly on flat ground. The Servites Church *Servitenkirche,* which is on this route, is a fine example of Baroque art.

66

Parish church interior, Innsbruck

The church was completed in 1654 and is built round a central clover leaf shaped rotunda. The clock tower was added in 1740. From the bridge there is a good view of the whole church. A passageway links the church to the monastery, which is now a seminary for the Servites who are a religious order who consecrate themselves to the upkeep of the pilgrimage sanctuaries in Austria.

Dividing grilles bar much of the church but glimpses of the fine paintings may be seen. The painting over the altar is of St Charles Borromeo, who was the patron of the church. The old road rather than the motorway is a more attractive route to the east. Volders, Wattens and Weer, where there is a campsite, all lie on this road. Three kilometres further along, at the hamlet of Pill, there is also a campsite and this is only three kilometres from Schwaz. All lie on the bus route along the main road and on the railway line.

Schwaz is interesting as it was hereabouts that the rich finds of silver were made which made the moving of the mint from Meran a sensible proposition.

Old houses (Old Town), Hall in Tyrol

Between the fifteenth and sixteenth centuries the mines were in full production and the town was very prosperous indeed. At that time it had the highest population of any town in the Tyrol except Innsbruck. The population today is about eleven thousand.

There are several interesting buildings in and around the town. In the summer there are weekly concerts in the hall of the cloisters of the Franciscan Monastery. The cloisters are open to view from the south side of the church.

It is pure Gothic in style, and there are remains of wall paintings dating from the sixteenth century. Various shields of craft guilds and miners' guilds are shown as well as paintings on the vaulting which date from the seventeenth century.

The Franciscan Church, *Franziskanerkirche,* was finished in 1515 and is laid out with three naves in accordance with the Order's own building rules. A notable feature is the Renaissance stall dating from 1618, which is the work of a local craftsman.

As befits a prosperous town, the
parish church reflected that prosperity.
Dating from the fifteenth century, it was
restored early in this century to its
original Gothic style with network
vaulting. There are four aisles and two
chancels. Of particular interest is the
elaborate Gothic decoration of the
vaulting supporting the organ loft, and
the Baroque organ case is beautiful. The
font dates from 1470.

In the south aisle there is a very fine
piece of religious sculpure, the altar of St
Anne, dating from 1733, with St George
and St Florian, the patron saints of
Austria, framing a sixteenth-century
group of the Holy family with St
Elizabeth and St Ursula. The church

also has two west doors, one of which
was for the exclusive use of the miners.

On the outskirts of the town, to the
south-east, is the Castle, or *Schloss,*
Freundsberg. This attractive castle
which sits boldly on the castle mound is
now the town museum, and the exhibits
trace the history of the town, which
dates from the twelfth century, and the
mining industry.

Open air and covered tennis courts are
available, and there is a heated open air
swimming pool. Riding is available in
the nearby hamlet of Pill. A chair lift in
three stages goes up to the nearby
summit of Kellerjoch, which is 2,344
metres high. Fifty kilometres of footpaths are cared for by the local council
for the benefit of tourists.

5 North, South and East of Jenbach

By way of the main road, number 171, or the minor road through the hamlets of Buch and Schlierbach, by rail or bus, Jenbach is not far from Schwaz. The town is at an important crossroads. South is the Zillertal, well known to many British holiday makers. North is the Achental, a beautiful valley going up to the German border at the Achen Pass.

The journey up to the valley, which levels off after the four hundred metre climb from Jenbach, can be made by bus, train or road. Jenbach in the main Inn valley lies at 562 metres, and the surroundings of the lake, up to the hamlet of Achental, are about 920 metres.

There is a delightful rack and pinion railway, steam hauled, which runs between its own station, alongside the main railway station in Jenbach, and the lakeside station two kilometres short of Pertisau. Buses run from Jenbach to the German border.

This hanging valley will be of interest to geographers. The waters drain north into the Isar and not south into the Inn. A barrier of glacial moraine created when the Inn valley was carved by its glacier is the explanation.

There are at least four campsites around the lake and five spots from which lake bathing is possible. Lake steamers ply the full length of the lake which is the largest, and some say the

Achensee

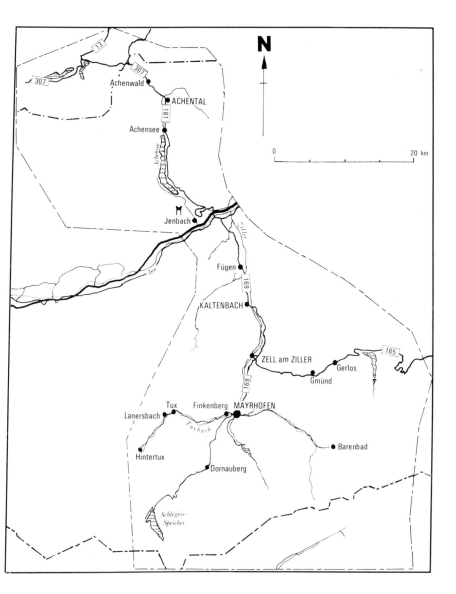

most beautiful, in the Tyrol. It is almost ten kilometres long and a kilometre wide at its widest point. In places it is nearly one hundred and fifty metres deep and the massive mountains of the Kar-wendel, to the west, and Rofans, to the east, rise almost from the shores.

On the way up splendid views down the Inn valley unfold and higher up mountain views are revealed.

Lying off the main road (No 181) though not the minor road from the centre of Jenbach, is Eben. Here in this tiny hamlet is the church of St Notburga, who is revered in the Tyrol as the patron saint of servants.

Achensee Railway and steamer terminal

The Achensee and Pertisau

Achensee from the Zwölfer kopf

Only a kilometre north is Maurach; in the area there are two campsites, facilities for all water sports, including fishing, and if the weather is inclement there is an indoor swimming pool. Tennis, bowling, cycle hire and minigolf are also available. At the information office a small local map of the footpaths in the area is obtainable. As Maurach lies right at the south-west foot of the Rofan group of mountains it has a cable car, of course. This goes up from near the centre of the village, 958 metres to 1,834 metres. Here the Rofan Mountain Hotel can be found, and alongside there is Erfurter Hut, an alpine club hut. Both have sun terraces overlooking the lake. Once this height is reached there are some good paths around the summits, the highest of which is the Hochiss, at 2,299 metres.

The main road to Germany goes along the eastern bank of the lake. The road on the western bank ends at Pertisau. The village stands on a level section of land just below the ends of two valleys. All watersports are available, of course, including fishing; the lake steamer calls at the pier; there is

tennis, indoors and out; and in the evenings one may play by floodlight. There is a nine-hole golf course here in delightful surroundings.

Behind the village the walk up to the Falzturnalm, a guest house, is delightful. It is more like a park than the open woodland it really is. Seats are provided for resting in the shade of mature trees of all kinds. The really hardy can go on to the Gramaialm, a large hotel with a farm nearby, and then on to the Lamsenjochhütte, 1953 metres. However, this is a long walk and over the last stretch, a tough one. Cars can be driven up to the Gramaialm but the buses turn round at Pertisau.

At the foot of the lake — remember the water runs north into the Isar and Germany — is the village of Achensee which spreads along the old road. The new high road takes all the faster through traffic, and joins onto Achenkirch.

There is a lovely campsite right on the lakeside with its own bathing place. The villages have twenty-five pensions and seven hotels, between them.

There are all the usual facilities for

*

**

73

water sport including rowing boats. (There are no motor boats allowed on the lake.) Other activities include tennis, minigolf, bowling, riding and fishing, either on the lake or the river, and plenty of local footpaths for walks, for which the information office will supply a small map. There is also a chairlift which will quickly take visitors to a height of 1,400 metres on the slopes of the Hochunutz, at 2,075 metres. The town band plays on some evenings, and the hamlet is not short of general evening entertainments.

Achental is the next hamlet and here there is a junction. A road leads off to the east, to the tree-covered hills and to a haven of peace and tranquillity. Steinberg-on-Rofan is a hamlet set deep in the hills to the north of the Rofan Mountains. As there is no through road, (there is a track out to the east and it is just drivable) the village enjoys quietness. Of course your morning sleep may be disturbed by cow bells or a tractor engine, but there is no other noise.

The last village is Achenwald, and it is at this point that the road and river part. The road soon climbs to the Achen Pass, taking the easiest route northward. The river, like all rivers, takes the easiest way down. It flows into a reservoir in Germany, the Sylvenstein, which is on the course of the Isar.

One of those anomalies found in mountain country lies a little way west. By following the road past the reservoir to Vorderris and turning south, the hamlets of Hinterris and Eng can be reached. Though they are both in Austria the only road access is north through Germany.

Hinteriss, where the Belgian royal family sometimes holiday, has a few houses grouped round a nineteenth-century hunting lodge. The area is a nature reserve and an area where chamois may easily by seen. There is a modern guest house/restaurant, and even a filling station. Plenty of gentle footpaths go round the area at modest level, though there are also high level paths.

Higher up the Engtal valley, is the hamlet of Eng itself. Here a collection of holiday chalets line the end of the road and there is a large modern guest house/restaurant. There are many visitors from Germany at the weekends, who climb the good paths south-west to the Binns Alm or even higher to the Lamsenjoch hut, which stands at the head of the Falzturn valley south-west of Pertisau. Joch means pass and from Eng the hut is just the other side of the Lamsenjoch, at 1,938 metres. To the west, also on a good path, is the Falkenhut, a climb of 590 metres. This is a fine walk giving splendid views of some of the peaks of the Karwendels and a massive limestone wall ahead soon after the start. The paths are good and safe and at all the huts and alms refreshments and accommodation is available.

Back down in the main valley is Jenbach, an unremarkable town not even listed in many guides, possibly because of its proximity to other more famous places like Innsbruck, Achensee and Mayrhofen. This small town lies just north of the motorway. It has an open air swimming pool and an information office and main line trains and buses.

Two kilometres south-west on the old road to Stams is Schloss Tratzberg. This gem among castles must be visited. The beginnings of Tratzberg are almost in the realms of legend, the records are so few. The first mention of the castle builders was in 1149, when the Rottenburg masters were squires to the Counts of Andechs. Two brothers of the Rottenburg line disputed about which ruling house to follow, Hapsburg or Bavaria. One took over Rottenburg, which is across the valley and now a ruin; the other brother built Tratzberg, out of spite it is said, and the name is derived from *'trotzen'* meaning 'to defy'.

Probably the castle was built on the original defensive position, a little to the east; first mention of the building is in 1288. The castle had many owners and varying fortunes. In 1847 it finally passed into the hands of the Counts of Enzenberg, who still own it. It is due to them that previous neglect and decay has been halted and restorative work undertaken.

In 1500 the old castle was pulled down and rebuilt by the owners of that time. A stone-carved coat of arms in the tower stairway reads '1500 Veit Jakob and Simon Tänzl, brothers did build this castle.' However, their fortunes changed and the Ilsungs became the new owners. This latter family continued the lavish decoration, but with a difference. The Tänzls built and decorated in Gothic style, the Ilsungs in Renaissance.

During a period when the Fuggers owned the castle they had the courtyard decorated. All the decorated facades are signed PD 1600 and are attributed to Peter Donner.

THINGS TO DO ROUND ACHENSEE

Steam cog railway, Jenbach to the lakeside.
Lake steamer trips.
Fishing at all resorts and at the river at Achenkirch.
Bathing in the lake or indoors at Maurach.
Tennis, bowling, minigolf, walking, Nine-hole golf course at Pertisau.
Cable car at Maurach. Chair lift at Achenkirch.

To visit the castle take the minor road from Jenbach to Stams. Two kilometres outside town there is the guest house Schlosshof. From here the visitor must make a twenty minute walk up a neat path through the woods past the outer bastions and terraces.

Only a part of the large castle is open to view; even so it is not possible to describe all that can be seen. The first room on view is the hunting room containing lifelike groups of animals carved by a local from Achental, Toni Steger. Many of the rooms are named after the Fugger family. The Fugger parlour and the Fugger chamber can be seen, where rich panelling and furniture are the primary interest.

In the Hapsburg hall, sixteen metres by ten, are paintings of the Hapsburg family tree, consisting of one hundred and forty-eight figures in all. They are of great interest for the information they provide about the clothes of the sixteenth century.

Among other rooms is the queen's bedchamber, a splendid room which shows the culmination of the splendour of the Renaissance period during Ilsung family ownership. On the north-east corner is the castle chapel dedicated to St Catherine, consecrated in 1508. It is quite large. The altar painting is early Baroque and shows the beheading of St Catherine.

Finally the armoury is visited. Prolific records allow the development of the armoury to be traced. This was one of the largest in the country, although over the years many items have been lost in battles. Notable items are the two long chamois spears used by Emperor Maximilian.

A visit to Tratzberg is a step back in time. It has widespread reputation for its historical culture and of this castle it has been said that 'It ideally imparts a

The Ziller Valley

picture of sixteenth-century culture'.

One of the most delightful valleys and centres one could wish to find is the Zillertal. For many years this has been a favourite with many visitors from Britain. It is claimed to be the most typical Tyrolean valley. Musicians from the Zillertal were known in all the courts of Europe, and a group appeared in London in 1837 to perform during Queen Victoria's coronation celebrations. So captivated by them was the queen that many an English soprano found it expedient to learn the 'wild songs'.

Before 1805 the Zillertal was not in the Tyrol but came under the jurisdiction of the Bishops of Salzburg. Notice the difference in the 'onion domes' of the churches; there is a boundary between the red and the green tops.

Higher up, beyond the Gerlos pass, was a famous place for crystal, and many folk tales tell of mountain caves lined with crystal. Aquamarines used to be found in the area, but the Zillertal was famous for garnets.

Today musicians from the Zillertal are still famous, for singing and for harp and zither playing. On the first weekend in May there is a spectacular festival which dates back over four hundred years. This is the Gauder Festival and tourists in thousands flock to watch and to join in.

The lower reaches of the valley are broad and may disappoint those expecting alpine scenery here. First of the villages is Strass near Jenbach, then Schlitters and Fügen, Kaltenbach, Aschau and then Zell-am-Ziller.

Here the valley divides; the main valley goes on to Mayrhofen while the offshoot goes to Gerlos. At Mayrhofen the valley again divides, this time into four. Mayrhofen is the start of picture postcard land again; each of the side

---

THINGS TO DO AROUND JENBACH

Jenbach
Swimming pool.

Tratzberg Castle
A gem of sixteenth-century culture, for opening enquire at Jenbach Information Office or at the castle.

76

A village festival, Zell-am-Ziller

valleys cut deep into the Zillertal Alps and a high alpine road has been built to take motorists up to points for viewing many peaks over 3,000 metres.

However, Strass is at the bottom of the valley. It has an information office, and the first railway station on the way up the valley. Schlitters has an open air swimming pool near the campsite.

Fügen is a few kilometres further up the valley, which is still wide at this point. Here there are facilities for tennis, minigolf and table tennis, a swimming pool with a large sunbathing lawn near the campsite. Over ninety kilometres of paths are cared for with three hundred benches for resting and taking in the views. A cable car goes up south-west of the town, taking the more adventurous up for an attempt on the Kellerjoch, (2,344 metres) or the Rastkogel (2,745 metres). A cycle path, the Radwanderweg, has also been laid out. There are many hotels and pensions and an active night life.

Kaltenbach is another pleasant little village catering for winter and summer tourists.

*

Ziller Valley railway

For many the Zillertal starts at Zell-am-Ziller, a lovely little village about at the point where the valley begins to narrow. High spot for railway buffs here will be the old steam train. Sometimes there are scheduled runs between Zell-am-Ziller and Mayrhofen; it is even possible to rent the whole train.

Set in a wide open area is the heated open air swimming pool and its lawns. There are facilities for tennis, open air chess, fishing and cycle hire. One of the hotels has a swimming pool available to the public. There is an active night life with Tyrolean evenings, cellar bars, discotheques and brass band concerts.

Mayrhofen seems to be a centre that has everything from a conference centre to a baby sitting service, and a cinema to a forest feast. In between there is fishing, swimming at either the indoor or outdoor pools, tennis, riding, cycle hire

and bowling. There is a lively selection of evening entertainments at many of the hotels. There is even a cinema and six *Tanzlokale* places for dancing, again in the local hotels. The village claims two hundred kilometres of footpaths.

A pleasant, easy walk goes along the forest edge down to Zell-am-Ziller, (nine kilometres) and takes about two-and-a-half hours. One could arrange this to coincide with a return trip by steam train. This walk starts behind the Europahaus, the conference centre, and goes left at the end of the Dursten Strasse. Follow a field path to Eckartau, down through the village, to a sign-posted track to Ramsau. Turn down into Ramsau and right at the church, where a track leads to Zell-am-Ziller.

A high level walk can be taken by taking the cable car, *Penkenseilbahn,* to Gschössberg (1,787 metres). From the

The climb to the Fortschaglhaus near Mayrhofen

an easy three hours, walk, mostly terrace at the top there is a splendid view of the valleys round Mayrhofen, and the glaciers of the Zillertal Alps. A chair lift may be taken higher, to 2,005 metres, or the footpath (No 23) near the cable may be followed. A ridge path then goes south-westerly to a minor summit and on to Penken, at 2,095 metres. Nearby is the Penkenjoch Hut. Behind the hut the path turns slightly right and goes downhill. The path forks to the left. A further left turn takes a path down to the Mösingalm and the middle station on the Finkenberg chair lift. Here the lift goes down to Finkenberg, or the walk can be continued in this direction to the Penkenhaus, at 1,810 metres. A good footpath goes on to the Gschösswand for a return by cable car. The walk takes three hours on easy paths. However, one must allow time for taking in the splendid views. From the ridge on the higher sections of the walk, there is a general panorama view of the Zillertal Alps.

Finkenberg is an attractive place to stay. Quieter than Mayrhofen, this little village is the home of Leonhard Stock, the world famous Olympic champion skier. It lies just inside the Tuzertal, the furthest west of the four fingers of the valleys or grounds, *gründe*, fanning out from Mayrhofen. Finkenberg has a heated open air pool and facilities for tennis and bowling. There are also slide shows, evening concerts and, of course, the chair lift to the Penken. A walking programme is available from the information office.

Higher up the valley the village of Lanersbach has a cable car. Actually the cable car starts at the hamlet of Vorder-lanersbach and goes up to the Schrofen Hut, at 1,700 metres.

Hintertux is the last hamlet, at the head of the valley, and almost against the valley head wall. It is here that the cable car goes up to the permanent glaciers and snowfields that enable skiing to continue all year round. At an altitude of 2,660 metres the Tuxer-ferner Haus has a terrace facing south to the snowfields. The experience of sun-bathing beside a snowfield is almost unbelievable the first time. However, care must be taken not to burn; the air is cool enough to feel comfortable but thin enough to allow more ultra-violet rays through than most lowlanders are used to. The swimming pool at Hintertux is a thermal pool and the village is quite popular as a spa. It is also the centre of a tradition in woodcarving.

Many of the hotels have facilities for sports in the hamlets of the Tuxertal. At least one in Lanersbach has a swimming

---

THINGS TO DO IN THE ZILLERTAL

Tennis: Mayrhofen and Zell-am-Ziller.
Bowling: Madseit near Hintertux.
Steam Train: Zell-am-Ziller to Mayrhofen.
Riding: Mayrhofen.
Fishing: Zell-am-Ziller and Gerlos.
Swimming Pools: Schlitters, Fügen, Zell-am- Ziller, Finkenberg, Mayrhofen, Gmünd, Gerlos.
Cycle Hire: Zell-am-Ziller.
Sailing: Gerlos.
Kaltenbach, Zell-am-Ziller, Mayrhofen, Finkenberg, Lanersbach, Gerlos and Krimml.
Train service from Jenbach to Mayrhofen.
Bus services to the outlying valleys.
Waterfalls Krimml.

---

pool and one in the hamlet of Madseit near Hintertux has a bowling alley. All of the valley is a winter and summer paradise. Frequent bus services from Mayrhofen make access easy. Low level and high level footpaths abound for an easy stroll or harder hike, the tourist offices will provide small sketch maps of the walk.

An interesting walk can be taken from Hintertux. Take the cable car to the Sommerbergalm (2,080 metres); this is the changeover point for the higher section to the Tuxer-ferner Haus. Take the path to the Tuxer-Joch Haus, or the chair lift to the Tuxer Joch, 2,338 metres. Down the other side of this pass is Schmirn, in one of the side valleys of the Brenner Pass. From the Tuxer-Joch Haus take path No 323 down the Weitental, an area frequented by chamois. Lower down the stream plunges into a wild gorge and often a haze is thrown out by the waterfalls,

Round the lake, the road is private but walking is allowed. This is a magnificent high alpine spot surrounded by peaks over 3,000 metres high, snow capped all year round.

Considered the most picturesque of the 'grounds' is the Stilluppgrund. Buses run from Mayrhofen to the Grüne Wand Haus, (1,438 metres) at the head of this valley; cars are not allowed quite so far, only to the guest house Wasserfall. A fast glacier-fed stream tumbles over many waterfalls in a gorge before the valley widens and gives views of the surrounding peaks and glaciers.

The Ziller river, from which the Zillertal is named, flows down the last valley (or ground), the Zillergrund. Due east from Mayrhofen are the hamlet of Häusling, a few guest houses, and at the

Hinter Tux in the Tuxer Valley

making this a very attractive walk. This is an easy three hours walk, mostly energetic people can use path 324 to walk all the way up from Hintertux; the ascent will take about two hours.

Beyond the village of Domanberg the road goes through tunnels (the first is three kilometres long), and has a number of hairpin bends on its climb to the large lake named Speicher Schlegeis, at 1,780 metres. There is a car park near the lake beside the Dominikshütle (1,805 metres) where short strolls can be made to see the views. The whole of the drive gives magnificent views of the highest peaks of the Zillertal Alps. The Hochfeiler, at 3,510 metres, is south, in line with the lake, and to the east is the Grossem Möseler, at 3,478 metres.

Tux woodcarvings

The Gerlos Valley

roadhead the Bärenbad Alm. This climbs amid the magnificent scenery almost to the border of the neighbouring province of Salzburg.

At Zell-am-Ziller the road No 165 goes east towards Gerlos and the Gerlos Pass, (1,507 ,metres). Buses run from Zell-am-Ziller and special outings can be made to visit the Krimmler Waterfalls.

From Zell the road starts off through the hamlet of Hainzenberg, which is reached by a series of hairpin bends up a steep slope. The Gerlos valley is a hanging valley and the route over the pass is classed as a scenic route, as, indeed, is the whole Zillertal.

The main Gerlos valley is soon reached as is the village of Gmünd, which is typical of the area. There are facilities for tennis and an indoor and outdoor pool.

Gerlos lies in a secluded combe at 1,245 metres. This beautiful high valley is a popular area both in winter and summer. The road winds through pine forests and pastures and many visitors travel along this romantic route. Accommodation is not lacking; there are plenty of hotels and pensions. Comfortable low level walks in plenty take visitors through meadows and woods to the welcoming alms. A chair lift goes up to the Ebenfelder Aste, at 1,820 metres. From here the highest peak in the Kitzbüheler Alps may be ascended. Path No D2 goes first to the Isskogel, (2,263 metres) and continues, taking a left fork to the Kreuzjoch, (2,559 metres). The return may be made the same way. The path is not too difficult and the start is over wonderful alpine pastures, full of flowers in their season. Allow six hours for the round trip. Views from the summits are breathtaking. To the southeast is the Hohe Tauern range with many peaks over 3,000 metres.

Gerlos has four swimming pools, including a heated outdoor pool. Sailing is available with boats for hire on the nearby lake, and fishing also. A tennis court completes the scene. There are beautiful side-valleys to explore here

also.

A wide sweep round the Durlass-boden Dam starts the climb, with a second sweep climbing higher with a view over the lake.

The actual Gerlos Pass lies on the minor road at 1,507 metres; nearby is a chair lift to the Königsleiten. This was the original road; the new tourist main road goes even higher to the Filzstein-alpe, (1,628 metres) where there is a car park.

The return downwards is fast and round a series of hairpins. The first view is of the upper Pinzgau valley, and in particular the Krimml Falls. Next is a view of a landlocked lake, the Burg-wandkehre, and its remarkable hillock, the Trattenköpf. Just as the road sweeps round to enter a tunnel there is a car park

Gerlos village

Gerlos village

Gerlos village church

and a closer view of the falls.

It is possible to walk to the falls. Leave the car in Krimml to avoid a toll road. A broad path leads to the lower falls; three-and-a-half hours should be allowed for a full tour of the falls. The path climbs with many hairpin bends and side paths to viewing points of the cascades. After about one hour's walking a level pasture is reached, and a welcome pause can be made at the guest house Schönangerl. The Tauern Haus, a guest house, stands at the top of the falls. The falls higher up are bigger than the ones below the Schönangerl and it is worth the extra effort to see them. Altogether the Krimml Falls descend about 383 metres, or 1,250 feet; they are the highest in Europe. A raincoat is a good idea as the woods are misted with spray from the huge falls and cascades. The best time to view the falls is midday as then they are descending with the sun behind them. Before leaving Krimml, a visit to the parish church is worthwhile, as the Madonna is striking.

6 Detour Round the Grossglockner

The descent from the Gerlos Pass takes the road into Salzburg Province. However, a short detour enables one to visit one of the engineering masterpieces of Europe. The Felber Tauern Tunnel takes the road back south into the East Tyrol.

Having left the Zillertal Alps behind, road No 165 leads down the Oberpinzgau valley between the Kitzbühler Alps to the north and the Hohe Tauern to the south. The Hohe Tauern contains the highest mountain in Austria — the Grossglockner, at 3,797 metres. Tours are available from the nearby towns, or you may wish to drive over the magnificent high alpine road culminating in the pass at Hochtor (2,505 metres).

From Krimml the next village is Wald im Pinzgau where, in the late Gothic churchyard, are many headstones made of rare minerals. Pinzgau is the valley; it runs down to Mittersill and the young Salzach river flows through it. Swiftly growing in size, the Salzach flows to the east for some hundred miles or so before swinging north through Bischofshoven, then Salzburg. A few miles north, it forms the border with Germany, then it flows into the River Inn which in turn, in about fifty miles, joins the Danube.

Glockner Road. Parking near the Franz Joseph Haus and the Glacier lift

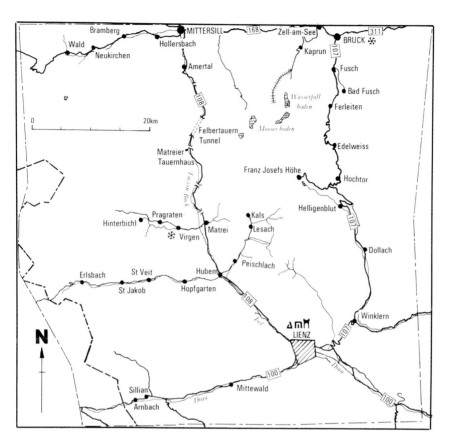

The Upper Pinzgau is an ideal holiday centre for those who cannot make up their minds whether to take a winter or summer holiday. In the main valley, the Salzachtal, when full summer has arrived and the meadows are wearing a coating of flowers, the side valleys are just in spring. The higher reaches of these side valleys are in eternal winter, with snowcapped peaks and all year round skiing. It is quite possible to ski in the morning and then play tennis or sail in the afternoon.

The road No 165 goes through the hamlets of Vorder Krimml, Wald im Pinzgau, Rosenthal, Neukirchen am Grossvenediger, Habach, Bromberg am Wildkogel, Mühlbach and Hollersbach before reaching Mittersill, which is just off a major crossroad.

Hollersbach and Neukirchen am Grossvenediger are main resorts for both winter and summer holidays, with all the usual facilites. Habach is at the foot of one of the main side valleys which cut south, deep into the high mountains. The Habachtal is the valley where once many emeralds were found. Examples of these fine jewels can be found in Salzburg Cathedral in the seventeenth-century monstrance, in the British Crown Jewels, and in the Hapsburg Crown Jewels in Salzburg Natural History Museum.

Recent attempts to start new works have not met with success. Fine emeralds have not been found for many years, although poor quality stones are still found.

The town is a winter and summer resort and has bus and rail links. It is also the local centre for hunting, a reputation it gained in the years between 1920 and the late 1930s, and which was renewed in later years.

South of the town the main road, No 108, climbs up the Felber and the Amer valleys. To the left is an area designated as a wildlife park, *naturschutzpark*. On both sides are breathtaking views of the Hohe Tauern range. Finally the road enters the Felber Tauern Tunnel.

In common with many tunnels and high alpine roads, a toll payment is required. The tunnels and high roads have, in many areas of Austria, been built mainly in response to the demand of tourism and trade. For example, much traffic flows through Austria en route from Northern Europe to the Middle East. Having been forced to build roads and tunnels in order to stop the through traffic stifling the country, the authorities reasoned that the through traffic should bear some of the cost. The same applies to the tourist traffic. The tolls are quite heavy, but compared to the cost of petrol for a diversion, not excessively so.

The Felber Tauern Tunnel is five kilometres long and is at an altitude of 1,600 metres. It makes the crossing from Salzburg Province to East Tyrol.

When the South Tyrol was given to Italy the East Tyrol was cut off and isolated from the North Tyrol, as the Glockner Pass is closed in winter. For a long time the East Tyrol became a backwater and the scattered inhabitants had to deal with serious economic problems.The tunnel changed all that and visitors can now gain easy access from the north on the all year round, all weather, road.

On emerging from the southern end of the tunnel there is a car park, and to the west up the valley is a magnificent view of the Grossvenediger (3,674 metres). A little further down there is a right turn to the Matreir Tauern Haus, a mountain hotel. From here it is possible to take a stroll, which lasts for about two hours for the round trip, to visit an unusual chapel at Aussergschloss. It lies beneath a huge rock, as do the remains of the hamlet of Innerschlöss.

Continuing down the valley, the Tauerntal, beside the river Tauern, the next village is Matrei in Osttiral. This is a picturesque town and a summer resort. The parish church is Baroque and attributed to Haganauer. Nearby is the Weissenstein Castle which is quite old but has been remodelled; it was formerly an outpost of the Bishops of Salzburg. In the thirteenth-century St Nicholas Church, *Nikolauskirche*, are some of the oldest preserved frescoes in Austria, also dating from the thirteenth century.

Matrei is a centre for climbing in the area and it also lies at the junction of the Tauern and Virgen valleys. Along this dramatic valley, which is only seventeen kilometres long, lie the villages of Virgen, Prägraten and Hinterbichl. All around are peaks of over three thousand metres, and this is a fine unspoilt valley, the higher reaches of which see the birthplace of the River Isel. None of these villages appear in tourist brochures, and are only visited by the Austrians and Germans, to whom it is a drive of only a few hours. The post buses reach them, of course, and there are information offices at Matrei, Virgen and Prägraten. Matrei also has a campsite, swimming pool and facilities for riding.

Huben stands guard at the next valley junction. Here are two valleys; to the west the Defereggental, and to the east

The Lienz Dolomites

the Kalsertal. Kals is the main village, and is one of the leading centres for climbing. At the very head of the valley is the Kalser Tauern House, a mountain inn. From the village below Kals, Lesach, a walk up the side valley to the Lesacher Alpe will reward the energetic with beautiful unspoilt mountain scenery; there are no chair lifts or cable cars. From Kals to the Kalser Tauern House the road runs northward and climbs, and the end of the road at the inn lies beneath the western slopes of the Grossglockner.

Back towards the main valley through the village of Peischlach and across the main road heading due west is the Defereggental, cutting deep into the Defereggen Mountains. Soon after

entering the valley there is a chair lift going northward onto a ridge where there are splendid views along the valleys and over the mountains.

Hopfgarten im Defereggen is the first village reached, after a climb, it is followed by St Veit and St Jakob, a small winter and summer resort and a marvellous example of a high mountain village.

Erlsbach is the last village, and until recently it marked the end of the road. Now, however, it is possible to drive on, up to the Staller Sattel, where there is a border crossing into Italy. It is possible to take a short cut back to Innsbruck. On joining the main road No 49, turn right towards Bruneck, continue towards Brixen but turn onto the road

No 12 at Schabs. This is the old road over the Brenner Pass, and it is much more interesting than the motorway, which is a toll road.

Having turned left (east) back towards Austria and crossed the border, the villages of Arnbach and Sillian greet the returning traveller into the Pustertal. Sillian is the highest village in the Pustertal, at 1,103 metres, and nearby is the powerful castle of Heimfels. This thirteenth-century castle is decaying, but it is worth a wander round the courtyards.

The river in the valley, which rises in Italy, is the Drau which, when it reaches Yugoslavia, becomes the Drava.

The road is good and the valley wide; there are good views of the Lienzer Dolomites to the south and the villages are picturesque. Well off the beaten track are the small villages. To the north, near the Castle Heimfels, a road cuts deep into the Defereggen Mountains to Innervillgraten where there is an information office for the out-lying area and villages. There is a campsite at Mittewald, which is only fifteen kilometres from Lienz. The so called sun terrace descends into this valley, high up on the north bank of the River Drau, with its tiny hamlets and small resorts and a network of delightful paths going deep into these romantic valleys.

Lienz is very old, but unfortunately has suffered six great fires in its history, the first in 1444 and the last in 1825. However, the town is delightful. The population is over 11,000 and it is the shopping centre for the East Tyrol. Visitors may be surprised to see palm trees growing in the street. However, the descent from the massive peaks and heights is dramatic. The higher peaks are to the north and Lienz gives the impression that southern Europe has begun.

Lienz lies at an important junction. One road is the route north into the Isel valley and the side valley which is still today one of the few remaining really traditional and unspoilt valleys of the Austrian alpine area. The other routes are the Hochpustertal into Italy, the high Grossglockner Pass and the Drau valley.

The Counts of Görz chose to live at Lienz and built the castle of Bruck, probably on the site of a Roman citadel which previously guarded the valleys.

Sights not to be missed in Lienz are the Lieburg Palace which dates from the

Lienz

The Lienzer hut in the Deben Valley

sixteenth century. It is now the seat of local administration, and is located in the main square. In the fifteenth-century parish church are four late Gothic altars, frescoes by Adam Mölk, and late Gothic tombs.

Schloss Bruck, Bruck Castle, lies just outside the town and is now the *Osttiroler Heimatmuseum,* East Tyrol Museum. Exhibits include finds from Roman excavations nearby, local antiquities, handiwork, folklore and paintings by the Tyrolean painters Albin Eggar-Lienz and Franz Defregger.

The castle dates from the thirteenth century and was partially restored in the sixteenth century; it is very well preserved. Among the outstanding features are the tower, the Knight Hall or *Rittersaal,* showing how the castle must have looked in medieval times, and the Romanesque Chapel. In the chapel are frescoes painted in the fifteenth century by Simon von Taisten, who worked on a number of churches in the Pustertal. The frescoes were commissioned by Count Leonhard and his wife Paula. Count Leonhard was the last of the line of the House of Görz; on his death the province passed to Emperor Maxmilian I, and became part of the Tyrol. There is a restaurant at the castle.

In the parish church, which fortunately survived the disastrous fires, are the tombstones, in Salzburg marble, of the Count and his wife. A large gallery in the town gives a

The Kerschbaum 'Alm', in the Lienzer Dolomites

PLACES TO GO IN THE UPPER ISELTAL

Walk from near the tunnel exit,
Matreier Tauern House to
Aussergschloss.
Walk from Lesach in Kalsertal to
Lesacher Alps.

Matrei in Osttirol
Swimming pool, riding.

Virgental
Unspoilt high alpine valley

Kalsertal
Visit the Kalser Tauern House a high
mountain inn below the
Grossglockner.

Defereggental
Chair lift, charming unspoilt
mountain villages.

Castle Bruck, Lienz,

comprehensive view of the work of Albin Egger-Lienz (1868-1926) whose work was often inspired by the inhabitants and the landscape of the Tyrol.

Lienz has two information offices and facilities for many sports. There is a cycle path, facilities for riding, bowling, tennis and minigolf. Walking is the great pastime, of course, at both low and high level, and many paths extend from the outskirts of the town into the pleasant woods.

Swimming is well catered for, and Lienz claims to have the most modern facilities at the Dolmitenband Lienz. Here there is a huge outdoor pool with large sunbathing lawns and an indoor pool close by with restaurant attached. Near the town is the small Tristach See, a lovely little lake with a lido providing facilities for bathing.

A cable car to the north-east ascends the slopes of the Zeltersfeld, (2,213 metres) and to the west a chair lift goes up the Hochstein. Good footpaths and mountain inns make walking in these mountains delightfully comfortable.

Lienz is a centre for climbing in the area and a rising winter sport centre.

The border with Corinthia is soon reached at the Iselsberg Pass, (1,204 metres), by taking road No 107 out of Lienz. However, before the border is reached, one finds the village of Iselsberg, which is a winter and summer resort. Details of its early history are still being discovered.

Diggings carried out in recent years have thrown light on the old See of Aguntum. On a hill jutting out into the valley are the remains of a fifth-century episcopal basilica, which was evidently built on the site of a smaller existing church. As the remains of a gateway and outer wall have been found it seems that the site served as a refuge for the inhabitants of the ancient town of Aguntum. In the Slav language the area was called 'desolate' and as this is patently inappropriate it can only refer to the desolation left by the invaders. These were the Avars and their servants the Slavs, who had swept away the town and its inhabitants. The Bishopric of Aguntum was last heard of in the year 604.

Descending from the Iselsberg Pass the village of Winklern marks the road junction where the Grossglockner road begins. The valley of the river Möll is broad and relatively flat, rising only gently until Heiligenblut is reached. Between Winklern and Heiligenblut there are five villages and three campsites. It is possible, from many centres around the mountains, to take coach trips over the Glocknerstrasse. Heiligenblut is in a dramatic setting when viewed from the south. It clings to a tiny outcrop of rock with its church as the most outstanding building.

The Iselsberg Pass

The Grossglockner High Alpine road
is an engineering achievement second to
none. Building this section of road
improved communications somewhat.
Previously there had been no crossing
between the Brenner Pass and the
Radstädter Tauern Pass, and these were
more than 160 km apart. However,
those magnificent engineers and
travellers, the Romans, used to keep the
pass open all year round. No-one has
since equalled this achievement.

Depending on the weather it is open
between mid-May and mid-November,
but a late or early snowfall may close the
road for a few days. Indeed, snow may
fall at any time of year on the higher
reaches, but in mid-summer it is not a
problem and the roads remain clear.

The route used by the Romans was
slightly different from that used today,
but when engineers were blasting to
build the Hochtor Tunnel they found a
Roman statuette. Appropriately the
statuette was of Hercules.

Döllach is a minor resort both in
winter and summer. The other villages
cater for tourists also. Heiligenblut is a
natural stopping place. It takes its name
from the church, the spire of which is tall
and slender, pointing to the mountains,
and on this approach it stands out with
the great mountains as a backdrop,
forming a picture which tempts many
photographers. The church dates from
the fifteenth century when the monks of
Admont built it to perpetuate prayers in
the name of the relic of the Holy Blood,
Heilig-Blut. This relic was said to have
been brought to the church in the tenth
century by Briccius, an officer of the
Court of Byzantium, whose tomb lies in
the crypt. One of the greatest treasures
of the church is the awe.inspiring
triptych altar screen, one of the finest in
Austria. In the churchyard is a 'book'
with metal pages recording the names of
the victims of 'our mountains'.

Heiligenblut has one of the finest
mountaineering schools in Austria. In
summer months it is transferred to the
Franz-Josephs Haus. Both Dölach and
Heiligenblut offer facilities for riding as
well as mountaineering.

Soon after leaving Heiligenblut (1,288
metres), the toll gate of the mountain
road is reached. At an altitude of 1,913
metres there is a viewpoint at the
Kasereck, offering views back to the
Heiligenblut basin. There is a left fork to
Franz-Josephs Haus. Both Döllach and
ends in a long terrace, mostly hewn from
the rock, and there is a large mountain
hotel; the Franz-Joseph House, at an
altitude of 2,418 metres. A short walk
along the terrace provides a spectacle
not to be missed; a massive glacier lies
below. This is the Pasterze Glacier,
which has a flow of ten kilometres (six
miles).

Beyond the hotel a path, which begins
on the last platform (the Freiwandeck)
leads above the glacier. It is a ledge on
the cliff really, but it is quite safe, and a
round trip takes about one-and-a-half
hours which leads to another spectacular
viewpoint. The altitude makes most

View of the Grossglockner from the Franz Joseph height

people breathless so take it easy. Also at the Freiwandeck is a funicular railway, or *Gletscherbahn*, allowing a descent to the glacier itself.

Return from the Franz-Joseph Hohe to the road fork at the Guttal, where a left turn starts the climb again. There is a viewpoint near the southern end of the tunnel, the Hochtor. It is as well to note that parking on the roadway is an offence, so park only at recognized parking places.

At the northern end of the tunnel the highest point of the road is reached, at 2,505 metres (8,218ft). If your car appears to be labouring don't worry too much as it will probably be lack of oxygen. Nothing grows at this altitude except a few hardy mosses; even the grass has disappeared far below this level. Early visitors will find themselves

driving in a gorge cut from the snow in some places.

The road now descends past the Mittertörl Tunnel (2,261 metres), and ascends again to the Fuscher Törl (2,428 metres). Between the two is a bare stony landscape. For part of the way the road runs along a corniche above the Seidelwinkl valley and there is an impressive view to the east.

A right fork leads up to the Edelweiss Spitze, (2,577 metres), where it is possible to park and obtain refreshments.Here there is a walk, which at an altitude of 8,000ft, (2,500 metres) requires care. The journey may be broken by a stop at the observation tower, where one can sit on the terrace and admire the breathtaking view: thirty-seven peaks over 10,000ft (3,000 metres) and nineteen glaciers.

Mayrhofen

Eng, in the Karwendel mountains

Gross Glockner and Heilingenblut

The Grossglockner

The descent now starts in earnest and the views are spectacular and ever-changing as the road twists and turns. There are twenty-six hairpin bends on the route. After another corniche, the trees reappear; soon after, Piffkar, and a ravine, are reached. The last series of hairpin bends end with the short run into Ferleiten, a mountain hamlet (1,145 metres). Fusch is reached after the road crosses the river and the wooded gorge. The Bärenschlucht is negotiated on yet another, though shorter, corniche.

From Fusch to Bruck on the Glocknerstrasse is only seven kilometres. Bruck is in the Pinzgau valley and the road left the East Tyrol at Hochtor to re-enter Salzburg Province. Better known for its association with the Glocknerstrasse, Bruck is a summer and winter resort with a pleasant swimming pool, a campsite, and a famous view of the Fischorn Castle nearby.

The major tourist resort in this area is Zell-am-See, which is easily reached from Bruck. An excursion can be made to visit the Kaprun valley, through the gorge past the old ruined castle to the Kessel Waterfall, which is floodlit at night. A three-section cable car goes up to a height of almost 3,000 metres to the Kitzsteinhorn, where there is year-round glacier skiing.

The town is situated where the valley broadens; beyond the town the road rises between steep mountains. Ahead, suddenly, looms the wall of the Limberg Dam, *Limbergsperre*. Kesselfall Alpen House marks the limit of access for cars and a bus shuttle service connects with the funicular to the dam. On the upward journey there are views of the valley and the dam. Above the Limberg Dam is the Mooser Dam; there is a complicated system of piping the water to the power station below the dams and pumping it back into the Wasserfallboden Lake Reservoir. The Kaprun Power Station machine rooms are open to visitors. A pathway along the top of the first dam gives a surprising and excellent view of the water of the Wasserfallboden below and the valley beyond. This is an interesting excursion round the lakes and the power station, and a spectacular

HIGHLIGHTS OF THE
GROSSGLOCKNER STRASSE

Döllach
Riding.

Heiligenblut
Riding, parish church.

Franz Joseph Hohe
A walk to a viewpoint. Funicular to the glacier, viewing terrace, car park.

Edelweiss spitze
Car park, walk to a viewing terrace.

Ferleiten
A mountain village.

Fusch and Bad Fusch
Mountain villages.

Bruck
Swimming pool, famous view.

one if the chair lift is taken. Views of the mountain ranges of Grossvenediger, the Wetterstein, the Karwendel and Kaisergebirge, and the lake at Zell-am-See can also be seen. Kaprun also has facilities for mountaineering, a good swimming pool and a campsite.

Further up the main valley are the typical villages of Piesendorf and Walchen. Niedernsill is just off the main road opposite Steindorf. Lengdorf and Uttendorf follow, then Stuhlfelden just below Mittersill.

All these villages are picturesque and offer the usual facilities for visitors — cafés, restaurants, hotels and varying evening entertainments.

Mittersill is a winter and summer resort and is the road junction that marks the return into the Tyrol, after a most spectacular and adventurous trip round the Grossglockner high mountain road and the lovely peaceful valleys of the East Tyrol.

7 Kitzbühel, the Brixental and the Inntal

From Mittersill road No 161 leads towards Kitzbühel, climbing to the Thurn Pass and the regional border. On the pass, which is only 1,273 metres, there is a refreshment stop, and a chance to park the car and stroll along the path to take in the view. To the west is the Oberpinzgau valley and due south is the Hollersbachtal, cutting deep into the Hohe Tauern.

Jochberg is the first village on the green slopes above Kitzbühel; a pleasant village widely spread out on the gentle slopes. The heated swimming pool is in a delightful setting and the sunbathing lawn has plenty of mature trees dotted about giving it a parklike appearance.

There are tennis courts and sixty kilometres of marked paths in the splendid surrounding area.

A pleasant round walk in the area starts at the end of the forest road just south of Jochberg. There is a right turn at the Hechenmoos onto a forest road, After four kilometres take path No 712. After about thirty minutes, the Gruber Alm is reached, and then the path goes beyond the alm to the Kelchalm Berghaus, a mountain inn at 1,432 metres. The path climbs further, past a turning to the right, and on to Karzum Tor, at 1,931 metres. Descend south to the picturesque Torsee, and then turn north-west to climb again to the

**

View of the Wilder Kaiser from the Hahnenkamm, Kitzbühel

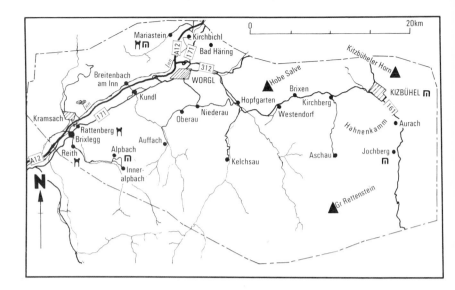

Gamshag, at 2,178 metres. The return journey passes the Schlictenalm and the Nieder-kaseralm. The path doubles back to the south before crossing the stream in the valley and returning to the starting point. Six hours should be allowed for the walk, which is moderate.

The village of Aurach has two parts, lower and upper. It is the next village down the valley from Jochberg. There is a right turn towards Oberaurach; the Auracher *Graben,* or trench, continues past the village. The Natur und Wildpark Aurach is four kilometres away along a good road. A sharp left turn on the valley road takes visitors to the wildlife park. The animals live free in the park; there are red deer with splendid antlers, wild pigs, a special breed of Hungarian sheep and many other animals. In the summer months there are occasional demonstrations with falcons and eagles. The information office in Jochberg will be able to supply opening times before a visit.

Kitzbühel is only about four kilo-metres down the valley. It is an old world town in a magnificent setting

between the Kitzbüheler Alps to the south, and the Kaiser Mountains to the north. It has been a fashionable resort for many years. Long before the heyday of winter sports, visitors came because of the unmatched scenery and the warm waters of the Schwarzsee nearby.

Possibly many people will think of the town as a ski resort, which in winter it certainly is, as the famous ski run of the Hahnenkamm is just to the south. Indeed, it is possible to ski eighty kilometres downhill, and by careful use of ski runs and lifts, there is no need to climb under your own power. In winter the tourist has the use of 56 cable cars or ski lifts, 60 ski runs, cross country tracks, bobsleighs and ice hockey and 250 ski instructors. The town was the birthplace of Toni Sailer, who was triple champion at the 1956 Olympic Games. At the height of the ski season, many famous faces can be seen around the town, as several celebrities have their own chalets nearby. Other events in winter include

---

View over Kitzbühel to the Hahnenkamm

*Schwarzsee and
Kitbüheler Horn*

skating, ski races, fancy dress balls and festivals. The main roads are kept clear of snow but the side roads are not salted, to avoid 'spoiling the winter scene'.

For the summer visitors there is plenty to do and see. Fishing, riding, bowling, tennis on any of the twenty tennis courts. There is an indoor ozone swimming pool, or lake bathing in the Schwarzsee. Boating is also available and there is a lakeside campsite. There are also facilities for golf.

An area walking programme is available from the information office and there is even a senior citizens' walking programme suitable for a steadier pace. Also obtainable from the information office is the 'summer holiday pass', *sommerferienpass*. This lasts for six days and gives worthwhile reductions on the cable cars and chair lifts, and free entry to the indoor swimming pool in the pump room.

One of the cable cars , north-west of the town, ascends in two stages to the famous Kitzbüheler Horn (1,996 metres), with its equally famous views. It is a mountain panorama and, on clear days, the very large lake Chiemsee, which is in Germany and over thirty miles away due north, can be seen.

PLACES OF INTEREST ROUND ABOUT
KITZBÜHEL

Jochberg
Walking programme, swimming pool tennis.

Aurach
Wildlife park.

Kitzbühel
Walking programme, golf, outdoor and indoor swimming, tennis, riding fishing, boating and bowling. Cable cars and chair lifts. Church of Our Lady, parish church, local museum (closed Sundays and holidays). Main line railway and local and distance buses.

Reith
Boating, fishing, lake swimming.

Kirchberg
Swimming, tennis, chair lift.

Kitbühel cable car to Kitbüheler Horn

It is quite possible to walk down, following the trackway, (but shortcut the bends), to the guest house Alpenhaus Kitzbüheler Horn (1,670 metres), then on path No 24 to the Pletzeralm near the cable-car middle station and the beautifully situated Adlerhütte, at 1,266 metres. Here a path goes directly down, or one can walk to the guest house Hagstein (1,032 metres) and so down to the outskirts of Kitzbühel. It is an easy walk requiring about two hours for the descent.

Within the town itself, which is over 1,000 years old, the main points of interest are in the old centre part of the town. The Vorderstadt and Hinterstadt are pedestrian precincts and have Bavarian-style substantial houses, often with paintings on the walls, making a

very picturesque scene.

There are two churches of interest. The parish church, *Pfaffkirche,* is on a raised site and has a tall slender tower and a mountain-style overhanging roof. The triple nave is fifteenth-century Gothic. In the Chapel of St Rosa of Lima the ceiling paintings were done by a member of a local family of artists, Simon-Benedkit Faistenberger (1695-1759).

The Church of Our Lady (Liebfrauenkirche) is distinguished by its massive square tower which houses a sanctuary. Simon Benedkit painted the vaulting in 1739 with a picture of the Coronation of The Virgin. Reminding the visitor that the church was an important place of pilgrimage until the nineteenth century is a painting of Our Lady of Succour

(Maria Hilf), which was painted in the seventeenth century. The local museum is well worth a visit. Among the exhibits is a cross-section model of the local silver mines. In their day they were the deepest in the world. Part of the museum is dedicated to the early days of skiing and includes early photographs and equipment. Evenings in Kitzbühel are, of course, well catered for. The town has a casino. The local town band performs on some evenings, and there are all the usual and varied entertainments.

Only five kilometres from Kitzbühel, and in a broad green valley, is the lovely little village of Reith. Lying on a minor road, it is convenient for the town while offering a more peaceful environment. It is three kilometres from the Schwarzsee and arrangements can be made in the village for fishing, boating and outings by minibus.

Road No 170 passes the turning for Reith, and goes up the Brixental. First village on route is Kirchberg, a pleasant village with a bathing lake and heated pool alongside. It has fifteen tennis courts among its facilities, and is on the train and bus route.

South from Kirchberg is the Spertental, with the village of Aschau at the end of the surfaced section of road eight kilometres from the main road. The valley cuts deep into the Kitzbüheler Alps. From the end of the unsurfaced road at the Labalm, four and a half kilometres beyond Aschau, it is possible to ascend the Grosse Rettenstein, at 2,362 metres. This marks the boundary between Tyrol and Salzburg and is one of the higher peaks of the range. The walk is suitable only for experienced mountain walkers.

Below Aschau, about one kilometre into the valley, is the valley station for the Gaisberg chair lift. From the

mountain end of the lift the summit of the Gaisberg can be easily reached in about two hours, by paths 2 and 2a to the Bärsättalm (1,451 metres), then path 11 to the summit (1,767 metres). This is a good walk in a quiet pleasant valley. Another five kilometres on up the main road is Brixen im Thale, which caters a little more for the tourist than Kirchberg. Here there is a splendid outdoor heated swimming pool and no less than twenty-three tennis courts with five indoors in the tennis hall. There is a walking programme, and a free programme of guided walks, both on the hills and in the lower regions. Band concerts and the usual evening entertainments are available.

The Sennberg *Sessellift,* or chair lift, goes up to Hochbrixen, where there is a splendid view of the whole of the Brixental. It is possible to walk back down. There is also a tiny lake, the Erlensee, where fishing is allowed.

Westendorf lies just off the main road, a little higher on a plateau. It is a winter and summer resort and has an active programme of evening entertainment and band concerts on Sunday evenings. The swimming pool and the sunbathing lawn are enormous and there is a programme of walks through the meadows and on the gentle hills to the south-west of the village.

There is a turning left, off the main road, into the delightful small village of Kelchsau. In the village there are some interesting traditional wood houses; one or two even still have the traditional shingle roofs held down with large boulders, something that is more often seen in the more mountainous regions. At the end of the surfaced road, beyond the village, there is a fork where the valley divides. To the left is the Short Ground, *Kurzer Grund,* and to the right the Long Ground, *Langer Grund.* Both

***

valleys cut deep into the Kitzbüheler Alps with the stream in the Long Ground, the Kelchsauer Ache, rising high up near the Kreuzjoch (2,558 metres), which is more than fifteen kilometres from the fork. The river is used by white water canoeists. There is a heated swimming pool in the village.

The turning into the Kelchsauer valley is almost at the outskirts of Hopfgarten, a stately market town in beautiful surroundings. Hopfgarten prides itself on the profusion of flowers in the town and, though of modest size, there is evening entertainment in the two modern cafes and in other establishments, Riding, tennis and mini-golf are available, as is a swimming pool.

In the centre of the town is the twin-towered parish church of St Jakob and St Leonhard, the 'Proud Cathedral of the Farmers'.

Near the foot of the chair lift there is a car park. The chair lift goes up to the Hohe Salve in three stages from 621 metres in the valley, 1,156 metres at the

first station, 1,532 metres at the second station, where there are excellent views, to 1,827 metres at the top. Refreshments are available near all three stations. The views from the summit are even better than the excellent views lower down. The view widens to include the more distant snowcapped peaks.

Just off the main road is a tiny hamlet with a history going back 1,000 years. Itter was started in AD902, and was originally in the Regensburg See until 1380 when it came into the care of the Archbishop of Salzburg. Today the castle is a luxury hotel, and has been restored to some extent. Leading to the castle the street is full of guest houses and pensions, and nearby is a campsite. In the surrounding meadows there is a network of footpaths, and there is a swimming pool nearby.

A descent of one hundred and eighty metres in eight kilometres to Wörgl will find the Inn valley once again. Wörgl is a thriving small market town well situated in the Inn valley, with a nearby motorway and main railway line. It is a convenient centre for touring the surrounding areas.

Within the town, or nearby, are all the usual facilities for evening entertainment including band concerts. Daytime activities include riding and cycling. Not only is there a programme of guided walks but also guided cycle rides. Information concerning galleries and exhibitions of various sorts in the town can be obtained from the information office.

South-east from the town centre a minor road leads to one of those quiet, tucked-away valleys which are such a delightful part of this country. This is the Wildeschönau, a wonderfully romantic valley with three small villages. In order of approach from Wörgl they are Niederau, Oberau and Auffach.

PLACES OF INTEREST IN THE BRIXENTAL

Brixen im Thale
Tennis, fishing, walk programme, swimming pool, chair lift

Westendorf
Tennis, bowling, walk programme, swimming pool, riding, minigolf.

Kelchsau
Swimming pool

Hopfgarten
Tennis, riding, swimming pool and chair lift.

Itter
Swimming pool, Castle Hotel (tenth century).

Old farm in Oberau

Between them they offer a surprising number of facilities, including a mountain rural life museum which is very interesting. Near Niederau there is a small bathing lake and two chair lifts bringing the green wooded higher slopes within easier reach.

Anyone using the campsite between Wörgl and Kundl, (it is alongside the road No 171), can take a circular walk and visit a romantic gorge. From the campsite go south-west to the guest house Köfler, uphill to the guest house Zuaberwinkl then on mostly level ground to the village of Oberau. Go south-west to Muhlthal then north-west,

View of Oberau

gently downhill, alongside the river. After about two kilometres the valley narrows into the Kundler Klamm (gorge). Near the bottom of the gorge is the guest house Klamm, and a ruined castle just below. The road is rejoined

Oberau church

near Kundl. A footpath goes back towards the campsite just on the edge of the woods south of the road. The walk uses very good paths in delightful scenery. The distance is about sixteen kilometres (or about ten miles), which is a good day's outing at a gentle pace.

One of Europe's gems is Rattenberg, once a famous and rich mining town like its neighbour Schwaz. However, its mining period was comparatively short. Between 1500 and 1560 two million kilos of silver were extracted. The town is near a narrow section of the river Inn, and by exerting control over river traffic the town was saved. The unfortunate collapse of the mining industry meant that the town was quite poor, and missed the building of the Baroque era, which means that today it is an unspoilt medieval town, the smallest in Austria.

There are the ruins of a castle in the town, which may be visited. From the terrace at the foot of the tower there is an excellent view over the town, *Schlossbergspiele,* or concerts in the

---

PLACES OF INTEREST NEAR WÖRGL

Wörgl
Tennis, swimming, riding, walking, cycling. Gallery.

Wildschönau
Rural Life Museum. Swimming, riding, tennis, chair lift.

Rattenberg
Tennis, fishing and bowling. Castle ruins. Glass workshops.

Brixlegg
Tennis, swimming, fishing, health spa. Nearby ruined castle Kropfsberg. Castle Matzen.

Main line trains, buses.

---

castle, are held here occasionally.

The parish church alongside the bluff on which the castle stands is well worth a visit. It was constructed in 1473, in Gothic sytle, and blocks of pink marble were used externally. Inside, the two naves are of different lengths, the shorter and most southern has stalls against a windowless wall 'for the miners'. Most of the wall paintings are attributed to Matthäus Günter who also painted the pictures in the parish church at Wilten. His painting here of the Last Supper is worthy of note.

The High Street, where the medieval houses have plain façades decorated with window and door frames in pink marble, is also very interesting. Along with its neighbour across the river, Rattenberg is famous for engraved and finely modelled glassware.

Brixlegg is only a very short distance south and is the gateway to the Alpbachtal, a superlative valley. The way into the valley is by way of Reith. However, Brixlegg, itself has some interesting places to visit. Matzen Castle lies in the middle of natural parklike surroundings; it dates from 1176 and is well worth seeing. Almost at the entrance to the Zillertal is the ruined Kropfsberg Castle, which was built to defend it. It is a most splendid ruin and is worthy of a visit. Between these two, which are a little over two kilometres apart, are the castles of Lichtenwerth and Lipperheide which sit, one on each side of the road.

Brixlegg is something of a spa and has a hot mineral bath, *Minerlbad Mehrn,* where it is claimed the calcium sulphate waters cure diverse complaints. The parish chuch of Our Lady is worth visiting. Tennis courts are available in Matzenpark, there is also an open air swimming pool and fishing can be arranged. Evening entertainment follows the usual pattern with band concerts on some evenings.

Reith is quite small but is is welcoming to tourists. Voted by an international jury in Brussels 'the best flower decorated village in Europe', the residents obviously work hard to maintain the good appearance of the village. In the middle of the village is a small lake, the Reither See, where bathing is allowed. A chair lift enables visitors easily to visit the Reither Kogel, at 1,337 metres, where there are fantastic views both up and down the Inn valley and up the Zillertal. There are facilities for fishing and tennis and pathways for gentle strolling or hard walking, whichever one wishes. Evening entertainment in the village follows the usual course: there are band concerts, of course, but also a *bauern theater,* farmers' theatre, or folk group where everything is done in the traditional manner, and speech is often in dialect, as it was years ago. This provides an unusual and entertaining evening, even if one is at a disadvantage with the language.

Higher up the valley, the villages of Alpbach and Inneralpbach are fine examples of alpine villages; most of the houses are beautiful specimens of the art of building in wood. Coming up the valley, the guest house Achenwirt is below Alpbach and about five kilometres from Reith. Here is the start of the two-section chair lift, going up to 1,804 metres, and, making light work of the summit of the Wiedersberge Horn, at 2,127 metres. From here there is another spectacular viewpoint, a panorama taking in the Zillertal, the Stubai Glaciers, the Karwendel and Kaiser Mountains. There is a choice of paths back down for the energetic, with refreshments halfway at the Almhof.

At Lagerhause there is a sharp left turn and a short climb to Alpbach, while Inneralpbach is straight on. There is an

information office and they have a
programme of walks, for this delightful
area. In addition there is an indoor
swimming pool, tennis courts, evening
concerts and slide show evenings. At
Inneralpbach there is a rural life
museum which is very interesting. The
valley is a winter as well as a summer
resort and is possibly busier in winter
when eighteen ski lifts operate.

Back in the main valley, cross the
River Inn at Brixlegg for Kramsach,
which has a good reputation for its fine
glass works. In the town there is a school
teaching the art of painting, etching and
engraving on glass. Near the town is the
seventeenth-century Castle Achenrain
and five small beautiful lakes. There is a
sixth lake higher up beyond Mosen, the
Berglsteiner See. The largest of the lower
ones is the Reintaler See, next is the
Krumm See. All these three have
bathing facilities and adjacent guest
houses with the same name as the lake.
The lakes are on a plateau 100 metres
above the River Inn.

There is a campsite down by the river
near its junction with the Brandenberger
Ache. This flows down the valley past
the village; all have the name Brandenberg. The river actually starts in

Germany from two different sources,
and its confluence is in Austria, a few
kilometres north. It flows down through
some of the beautiful wooded valleys of
the Brandenberger Alps.

An easy walk of some eight kilometres
can be taken down the lower reaches of
the Brandenberg valley. Take the bus to
Brandenberg near the church, and take
the path down to the river. The village is
worth taking a stroll round first, as it is a
very beautiful setting surrounded by
woods. Cross the river by the bridge to
the west bank and walk downstream
through the Trefenbach Klamm on a
good path, then a track. This track
crosses the river again just outside
Kramsach at the hamlet of Mariathal.

At this point, but on the west bank, is
the valley station of the Rosskogel lift,
otherwise known as the Sonnwendjoch
Berg Bahn. The lift goes up in two stages
to 1,790 metres near the Rosskogel Hut,
where many visitors go for the higher
level walking over a grassy plateau and
then down to the Zireiner See, on a
good, wide safe path. Here is an alpine
jewel, a lake at 1,793 metres, set in a
grassy hollow with paths round about. It
marks the eastern limit of the Rofan
Mountains that the Achensee guards at
the western end.

Kramsach boasts sixty kilometres of
low level paths and ninety kilometres of
mountain path. Temperatures in the
Zireinsee will be lower due to the
altitude, but the lower lakes near the
village have a summer average
temperature of 22 to 26 degrees
Centigrade.

The opportunity to visit the *Freilicht-
museum Tiroler Bauernhof,* (open air
museum of Tyrolean farm buildings)
should not be missed. Here many typical
wooden houses and farm buildings are
preserved in a pleasant lakeside
meadowland. They have been carefully

rebuilt in this meadow, and are widely spaced for the best effect. They give a unique insight into the way of life of generations of mountain farmers.

By far the prettiest route northwards is the old road from Kramsach, past the lakes, on the northern bank of the Inn to the small village of Breitenbach am Inn. The motorway, the main road and the railway are all on the other side of the river, leaving this village in peace. It has a swimming pool and a network of footpaths for gentle walks, and evening entertainments for most tastes from band concerts to folk singers.

Still on the north bank of the river, eight kilometres from Breitenbach, there is a fork in the road. The right fork takes the road back across the river to Kirchbichl and Bad Häring. Bad means bath or spa and there is a *Kurhaus,* or pump room, though not on a grand scale.

The left fork goes over a ridge into a quiet valley and to the tiny hamlet of Mariastein. With a population of less than two thousand, the attraction which has drawn pilgrims, visitors and tourists for many years is the castle. When the

massive tower was built in the fourteenth century, its purpose was defence. The Lady Chapel became a place of pilgrimage and gradually this aspect became more important. From the castle court, stairs lead to the *Rittersaal,* Knights Hall, which contains the treasures of the castle, the crown and sceptre of the Counts of the Tyrol.

On the upper floors are two chapels. The lower one is the Chapel of the Cross, *Kreuzkapelle,* and this has a Gothic interior dating from the sixteenth century. The upper Chapel of Miracles, *Gnadenkapelle,* was redecorated in the nineteenth century when it was restored to the original Baroque. At the same time the windows were enlarged, thus improving the lighting. The statue of The Virgin dates from the fifteenth century.

Continuing northwards, Schloss Schömwörth is just outside Nieder Breitenbach, this and the next village of Unter Langkampfen are all within five kilometres of each other. The last named village is only eight kilometres from the centre of Kufstein.

KRAMSACH AND BRANDENBERG

Kramsach
Tennis, lake swimming, walking, chair lift.
Open air farm building museum.

Brandenberg
A quiet peaceful village.

Main line trains at Rattenberg, buses up the valley to Brandenberg and to the chair lift.

PLACES OF INTEREST ALONG THE ROAD TO KUFSTEIN

Breitenbach
Peaceful village, tennis, swimming pool, gentle footpaths.

Mariastein
Castle. Swimming pool.

On the bus route. Main line trains at Langkampfen.

8 Kufstein and the Kaiser Mountains

Kufstein is a medieval fortified town dominated by the massive *festung,* or fortress. The town lies at the centre of a delightful part of the country; mountain walking is made easier by the network of good paths penetrating the valley and ascending the peaks of the Kaiser Gebirge.

There are warm lakes for bathing not far from the town, and romantic woods and flower-decked meadows for walks.

To the east it is possible to make a circuit round the area known as the *Ferienwinkel am Kaiser,* or holiday corner on the Kaiser, which is a beautiful area of wooded valleys, quiet peaceful villages, lakes and rivers.

As it is only about two hours from Munich by motorway, the area is popular with the Bavarians, but is little known to British visitors who tend to go to the Zillertal, Salzburg or Zell-am-See. Bordered on the east by the Loferer and Leoganger Steinberg range, which form the border with Salzburg Province, on the north by Germany and on the east by the gentle Brandenberger Alps, it is an excellent area for a winter or summer visit.

The Kaiser Gebirge are really two ranges the *Wilder,* (or Wild), Kaiser to the south rising to 2,344 metres, and the

Kufstein fortress

The Gross Glockner

Innichen in the Pustertal

St Johann

Kufstein Fortress

smaller northern range the *Zahmer* (or gentle) Kaiser rising to 1,997 metres.

Geroldseck Festung was built by the Dukes of Bavaria in the twelfth century to guard the entrance to the Inn valley. When the fortress commander was

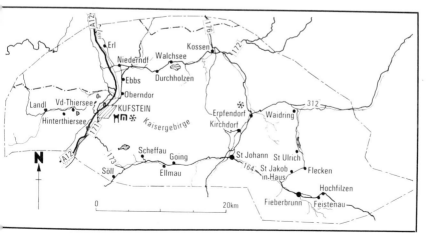

Old 'Gasthof' Kufstein

under siege by a Bavarian force in 1703 he had the town burnt to give him a clear line of fire. The fortress has fought off many sieges and on show are some of the guns and cannon used. Later it was used as a political prison, and the cells can be seen with mementoes of some of its famous prisoners. It is now the town museum, and English speaking guides are available. The immense Emperor's Tower is the larger, higher tower with walls four-and-a-half metres thick and built round a central column. It is encircled by a vaulted gallery. On one level are the guns and on a higher level the cells of the political prisoners. A deep well was bored in the rock; it is over sixty-eight metres deep. There is an ingenious way of raising the water, on a treadmill.

Also part of the fortress, in the Burghers' Tower, is the Heroes Organ, Heldenorgel, which is controlled from the gallery for the audience at the foot of the rock. It is claimed that on a still day the organ can be heard from a distance of eight kilometres. It was first played in 1931, having been built as a memorial to Austrian and German dead of World War I. Daily recitals are given at noon.

An approach to the fortress can be made from the near church in the Unterer Stadtplatz; a covered stairway goes beneath the Burghers' Tower. An

View of Kufstein from the Kaiser valley

easier approach is by lift from the riverside promenade. Following a tour of the
museum, which includes the Emperor's
Tower, it is possible to stroll around the
outer walls, where there are splendid
views of the district, across the river to
Pendling (1,563 metres), or east to the
Kaiser Mountains.

Kufstein has a smart shopping centre
spreading out from the Oberer Stadtplatz, and a romantic old street below
the fortress, the Römerhofgasse, which
contains the oldest winehouse in the
Tyrol, the Batzenhäusl. There are free
guided tours of the town which take in
the *Heldenhügel,* Hero's Hill, where
there is a statue of Andreas Hofer who
fought the French and Bavarians here in
1809. From the bluff there is a good view
of the position of the fortress.

As well as four bathing lakes there is a
swimming pool, tennis and a tennis hall;

fishing can be arranged; and there are
numerous footpaths, also four chair
lifts. The chair lifts make possible an
easy approach to the Kaiser Mountains,
but most of the peaks are for more
experienced mountain walkers. Paths on
the lower slopes are good and a local
sketch map can be obtained from the
tourist information office.

An idyllic tour west of Kufstein takes
in some of the most beautiful lake
scenery in the Tyrol. A bus service runs
to Hecht See from Kufstein, where there
is a beautiful lake with splendid facilities
for bathing and refreshments. A
footpath goes all the way round the lake,
just on the edge of the woods which
enclose the lake and its sunbathing
meadow. The walk can be extended to
take in the Egel See or the Läng See
which are smaller lakes, without
facilities, nearby. The ruined Thierberg

*

River Inn and Kufstei.

Castle is close to Läng See.

The hamlets of Vorder Thiersee, Hinter Thiersee and Landl are situated in this pleasant green valley. Furthest from Kufstein is Landl, a scattering of pleasant modern houses with a traditional church, a swimming pool, bowling alley and the smart Gasthof Zum Post. Hinter Thiersee lies higher and a little off the main road; here the church has a straight spire, not the more familiar onion-shaped dome. It is a pleasant village in broad meadows below the woodland climbing to the south.

Thiersee, village and lake, has boatin. and fishing facilities as well as lake bathing. A campsite is close by the lake shore and there are many facilities for refreshments.

Between them the villages boast three indoor pools, *Hallenbad,* two hundred kilometres of footpaths, three tennis courts, band concerts and a folk theatre

The climb to the Ellmauer Tor, Kaiser Mountains

for evening entertainment. Thiersee is also known for its passion play.

Performances of this play first began in the seventeenth century. It is re-enacted every six years, only being interrupted by World War II. A newly-built theatre, which seats nine hundred, is now its home. It is acted by a village amateur group, non-villagers are not allowed to take part. It was last performed in 1982.

To take a tour round the Kaiser Gebirge, leave Kufstein by the road south, No 173. Local folk tales tell of many spirits abroad in their region. Charlemagne supposedly lies buried beneath the Wilder Kaiser; in a cave there is a sleeping prince guarded by seven giants; beneath one of the peaks, the Totenkirchl (2,190 metres), there is a female giant. It is difficult to believe in all this in the peace and tranquillity of the high pathways.

Where road 173 meets the main road

A typical 'alp' with the Kaiser mountains

Town view, St Johann in Tyrol

312, turn right, for Söll, which is only two kilometres from the junction. The main part of the village lies back from the main road. A chair lift goes up to the Hohe Salve, at 1,827 metres. Altogether there are 120 kilometres of marked and cleared footpaths, with 500 seats. Splendid views of the southern aspect of the Wilder Kaiser, which shows very light-coloured in the sunshine, may be obtained from the village and surroundings.

All the usual facilities, including a guided tour of a farm, and evening entertainment are available, and the Moorsee is a delightful small lake easily reached from the village.

The next village on the tour is reached by turning north off road 312 on a minor road to Scheffau. Lying well back off the main road, and being on a no-through-road backing onto the mountains, this is a very quiet village and lays claim to having particularly pure air. The village is a good centre for walking, lying as it does at the centre of a network of paths. There is a swimming pool in the village, or one can go up to the Hintersteiner See. A most peaceful and easy walk is round the lake (the southern shore is tree lined); a forest road goes along the north bank to a swimming place and beyond to a guest house Widauer, which is the point from which to start the return journey. It is an easy walk of about two hours.

The next two villages, Ellmau and Going, again just off the main road, are typically Tyrolean. Ellmau has wooden fronted houses on the main street, and a charming little chapel. Going has a beautiful bathing lake, a walking programme and facilities for tennis, bowling and squash. All these villages, of course, have facilities for winter sports, but in the next few kilometres the road leads on to St Johann in Tyrol. This is the largest town in the area, the market town and holiday centre for this corner of Austria. Second only to Kitzbühel as a winter sports centre, it provides facilities just as good but, not being quite so fashionable,

---

PLACES OF INTEREST IN KUFSTEIN AND THIERSEE

Kufstein
Fortress, housing the town museum, the deep well and Heroes Organ. Guided town walks free. Chair lifts, swimming, fishing, tennis hall.

Thiersee
Bathing lakes, swimming pools, bowling, tennis, fishing and boating. Passion play every six years.

Main line trains at Kufstein. Buses to Thiersee.

PLACES OF INTEREST SOUTH OF THE WILDER KAISER

Söll
Swimming (indoors and out), riding, tennis, squash, bowling and chair lift.

Scheffau
Peaceful mountain village, walking centre, mountain lake, swimming.

Going
Swimming, riding, walk programme, bowling

St Johann in Tyrol
Swimming, fishing, riding, golf (nine or eighteen hole), bowling, tennis, cable car and chair lift.

Kirchdorf
Swimming, cycling, riding, fishing, bowling, tennis, walk programme.

Fieberbrunn
Lake swimming.

Trains to St Johann, via Kitzbühel, and on to Hochfilzen. Villages are on bus route.

---

it provides them at a lower price. To be fair to the rest of the Tyrol, every town and village has facilities which would more than satisfy the average visitors' needs. Not all of us could, or indeed would wish to, ski down the Hahnenkamm. The other famous skiing hill, the Kitzbüheler Horn, can be reached easily from St Johann. A funicular and a cable car make the ascent; the funicular goes up to the Anger Alm, (1,295 metres), and the cable car goes on up to the Harschbichl (1,604 metres). This is on a lower northern promontory from the summit proper and a saddle, slightly lower, must be crossed first if the summit of the Kitzbüheler Horn itself, at 1,998 metres,

Bringing the cows down from the high meadows, St Johann in Tyrol

is to be gained.

St Johann itself has splendid facilities for swimming, indoors or out, but if used as a centre the surrounding lakes may be reached in about twenty minutes by car and most are on or near the bus routes.

The town lies in a large flat area at the junction of two valleys. The setting means that as a centre it has the best of all worlds. Kitzbühel can be reached in twenty minutes, Kufstein in an hour, surrounding mountains in decidedly less. St Johann has a climbing school and a school for ramblers — mountain walking needs some expertise, though the town claims 100 kilometres of promenades and gentle paths and being in such a large open space it is possible, maybe uniquely for the Tyrol, to walk a surprisingly long way on the flat.

Not being content with one summer dry toboggan run, St Johann has a double one, *Sommerrodelbahn*. Little toboggans on wheels run down a half section concrete runway. The only control is a brake, steering is effected by the shape of the runway. A chair lift

takes the customer to the top of the run, where they are launched.

The town has guided walks and a special programme matched to the steadier pace of senior citizens. As a tourist centre St Johann has an active evening entertainment programme. There is nothing more pleasant after a day walking in the mountains than to relax on a terrace with a drink, and listen to the town band in concert from the open air pavilion.

In September there is a festival with a rather special event. In the Speckbacher Strasse a long table is set up right down the centre of the street on a Saturday afternoon for the Dumpling Feast, where dumplings are consumed in great quantity.

If St Johann itself is too large a centre to stay to explore the area then five kilometres to the north, on the 312 road, is Kirchdorf. The main part of the village lies off the main road in a broad valley with a glorious view of the east face of the Wilder Kaiser. Facilities for many sports can be found in and around the village, and they operate a walking programme. One of the walks must be to the Nieder Kaiser whether one starts from Kirchdorf or St Johann. This ridge extends far to the east of the main group and at its highest point is only 1,279 metres high, and mostly wooded, with a steep craggy slope to the south. At the eastern end near the fork in the path that leads to the main ridge is the Gmail-kapelle, and close by the Lourdes Grotte, the site of some miraculous cures many years ago.

To continue the tour, go south-east from St Johann towards Pass Griessen (963 metres), also called the Hochfilzen Pass after the village of the same name. It was near here, not many years ago, that during an army exercise, when the group guarding the border were being driven back by the group invading from Salzburg Province, the proud traditions of the Tyrol were upheld. Much to the amazement of a visiting observer, who said that he had never seen anything like it before, the locals turned out in force to repel the 'invaders'. Armed with pitch-forks, scythes and shotguns, the proud Tyroleans supported their defenders.

Between St Johann and the pass there are three villages, Fieberbrunn, Fiestenau and Hochfilzen. There is not much to choose between them. They are all pretty, and some claim Fieberbrunn to be the prettiest, but it is a matter of opinion. All of them have facilities for winter and summer holidaymakers in a splendid area in this quiet corner of the Tyrol.

Fieberbrunn has some history as a spa; people came to 'take the waters' as a cure. In fact the name Fieberbrunn translates as Fever Spring. Swimming is available at the small lake known as Lauchsee or in the heated outdoor pool or indoors in the the village.

There is a minor road going from Hochfilzen to Flecken, or it is possible to reach Flecken by returning past the right turn to St Jakob in Haus and so to Flecken. Just a little way along the road north is St Ulrich am Pillersee.

Its own claim to be 'an island of quiet' is true; the only reason to travel on this quiet road is to reach one of these three hamlets. St Ulrich is another gem, a hamlet really with its green-roofed church predominant against a backdrop of green hills. The lake is quite large, about two kilometres long, and has facilities for boating, windsailing and fishing. Apart from the facilities for high level walking in the Steinberge Mountains the area has a large number of level marked paths around the village. A favourite is the walk round the lake, and this will take about three hours. The opportunity should be taken on this walk to visit the Kapelle St Adolari dating from 1013, and also the *Teufelsklamm,* Devil's Gorge, where there is a lovely waterfall.

*

Should there be an odd wet day, there is a bowling alley and an indoor pool. St Ulrich also boasts a cure bath for asthma and neuralgic complaints.

Every guest attending the greeting ceremony for the incoming visitors, *Begrüssungsabend,* gets a free drink, the rather potent obstler which is akin to schnapps. St Ulrich is a beautiful, peaceful village in a lovely setting.

At the head of this valley, where the minor road meets the main 312 Salzburg to St Johann road, is Waidring, which is a picturesque hamlet with the central group round the fountain in the square being particularly noteworthy. Some of the houses still have the roofs of shingles held down by large stones and, of course, the balconies are flower decked.

Walking in the lovely woods and meadows is recommended and the village claims fifty-three kilometres of footpaths. There is a programme of

View of the Loferer Steinberg mountains

guided walks and the more adventurous, or hardy, may ascend the Steinplatte (1,869 metres), which is due north of the village and on the border of Salzburg Province. This walk is moderate and requires three hours. The walking route, *Durchkaser,* is an alpine path selected as a path for novice alpinists; the information office will supply details.

There is a wood carving school in the village preserving one of the traditions of the Tyrol. Facilities include a heated swimming pool, tennis courts and a bowling alley. There are band concerts on some evenings.

Eight kilometres past Waidring, heading west on the main road, (signposted St Johann) there is a road junction and the village of Erpfendorf. This small village, fortunate enough to be bypassed by the main road, is unremarkable on the whole in this land where most villages are so picturesque. However, students of architecture will want to stop to see the modern church, which is the work of Clemens Holzmeister, an Austrian master of contemporary religious architecture. The stained glass windows were finished in 1971 and other recent (some still unfinished) work includes mosaics in the chancel and a wooden rood beam showing the Crucifixion.

At this point St Johann is only eight kilometres south. To the north is the Kössener Tal which appropriately ends at Kössen. This is a pleasant drive of about eighteen kilometres along a good road which descends gently with the mighty river which here is called the Grosse Ache, though when it crosses the border into Germany just north of Kössen it is called the Tiroler Ache.

Kössen, with three other hamlets, is

Walchsee, the old town

situated on a large, mostly level, area at a junction of two valleys. This is a delightful spot to use as a centre, for a few days or an entire holiday. To the south is the chair lift going up in two sections to 1,690 metres. A path continues south to the summit of the Unterberg Horn (1,773 metres). A longer walk can be taken by heading south from the summit to the Lack-Alm (1,312 metres). There is a sharp right turn, and a descent down the side of the Niederhauser Tal. Cross the stream of the same name and follow it downstream to the guest house Kucknerhof. There is a right fork. The walk is ten kilometres long, nearly all downhill, and on good paths: it takes approximately three hours from the top of the chair lift.

To the north of the village the river passes through a wooded gorge, and a modern metal bridge carries a pathway across the river and creates a splendid vantage point.

The villages provide all the usual sports and evening entertainments; there is even a hang gliding school, and there is a folk theatre, band concerts and Tyrolean evenings.

Walchsee is a little way to the west; the lake and village share the same name. As one might expect with a warm water lake it is extensively equipped for water sports from bathing to waterskiing, boating to windsurfing. There is a windsurfing school, and an extensive network of foopaths around the area; it is possible to walk all round the lake and get an excellent view of the village from across the water.

The circuit of the Kaiser Mountains is now almost complete and the hamlet of Durchholzen marks the start of the descent back to the Inn valley. Six kilometres past Durchholzen the road forks. To the left (southerly), are the villages of Ebbs and Oberndorf, both with good facilities for visitors. The right fork goes to Niederndorf and Erl. All these four villages are in the main Inn valley in most beautiful surroundings, in broad green meadows with the mountains in the background.

The village of Erl must have special mention; this picturesque village is home to one of the oldest passion plays of the alpine regions. Its origins can be traced back to the religious plays which were first performed there in 1613. Not so internationally-known as Oberammergau, the audiences tend to be largely Austrians and Bavarians. However, recent seasons of the theatre have attracted over 100, 000 visitors. The passion play is produced every six years and will be performed in 1985.

In 1958 a new theatre was built just on the edge of the village, it holds 1,500 people. It has a varied programme including folk music, orchestral concerts and the world famous Vienna Boys Choir.

Having entered the Tyrol over the high pass from the Vorarlberg the tour is now complete.

PLACES OF INTEREST NORTH OF THE KAISER MOUNTAINS

St Ulrich am Pillersee
Swimming, tennis, bowling, fishing, boating.

Waidring
Swimming, tennis, bowling, fishing, guided walks.

Erpfendorf
Modern church, 1957

Kössen
Fishing, riding, swimming, bowling, tennis, cycle hire, hang gliding school, guided walks. Folk theatre.

Walchsee
Swimming, fishing, bowling, watersports.

Ebbs
Riding (with school), swimming, tennis, cycle path.

Oberndorf
Riding, swimming, walk programme.

Niederndorf
Swimming.

Erl
Swimming. Passion Play Theatre.

Buses: Waidring, St Ulrich, Erpfendorf, Kössen, Walchsee, Ebbs, Oberndorf, Neiderndorf, Erl.

Further Information

ON-THE-SPOT ADVICE

Almost all the towns in the Tyrol have a tourist information office (*Fremdenverkehrsverband*), where information about local hotels, campsites, excursions, museums, special events, etc may be obtained.

TELEPHONE CALLS

Telephone numbers consist of a three, four or six-figure number plus a four-figure prefix which is the area code. For calls made within Austria add the prefix 0; for calls from abroad add the relevant dialling code for Austria, ie from the UK add 01043, and from the US 01143.

TOLL ROADS IN THE TYROL

Tyrol/Italy
Brenner Motorway

From Innsbruck (Austria) to Bolzano (Italy). Only cars, minibuses and motorbikes are permitted on the Italian section of the road. Coaches, cars with luggage or caravan trailers and heavy vehicles are prohibited.

Timmelsjoch Alpine Road
Open: May-October.

Tyrol/Vorarlberg

Arlberg Road Tunnel

Silvretta Alpine Road
Open: June-mid-October. No cars with caravans or heavy vehicles.

Tyrol/Salzburg

Gerlosplatte - Krimml
Open: all year.
Toll-free on the Tyrolean side, toll payable on Salzburg side.

East Tyrol/Salzburg

Felbertauern Road

Tirol

Absam - Eichat - Halltal
Closed in winter. No coaches.

Aschau (see Zillertal road)

Ellmay - Wochenbrunner Alm
Open: all year, only cars and minibuses.
Toll refundable as refreshments at Gasthof Wochenbrunn.

Ginzling TWK (Tyrolean power works)
Open: May-October.
Private road to the Schlegeis reservoir.

Gnadenwald - Hinterhornalm
Open: May-November.

Grinzens – Keinater Alm
Open: summer only.
Cars and minibuses only.

Hinterniss - Eng
Open: May-November.
Reached from Germany.

*Hippach (*see Zillertal road)

Kaltenbach (see Zillertal road)

Kaunertal
Open: May-December.
Printz-Weisseeferner, from Gepatsch reservoir toll payable. Holders of ski pass free of charge.

Kirchdorf – Kaiserbachtal – Griesener

Alm
Open: Easter-early November.

Kitzbüheler Horn Mountain Road
Open: May-October.
Toll refundable as refreshments at
Alpengasthof.

Landl (see Thiersee - Landl -
Achernalm).

Matrei am Brenner - Maria Waldrast

Maurach - Achenkirch
Open: June-October
Old Achensee road.

Mayrhofen – Gasthof Wasserfall
Open: May-October.

Pertisau – Falzthurnalm – Gramaialm
(or Pertisau - Pletzachalm - Gernalm)
Open: May-October.

Ried/Zillertal (See Zillertal road)

*Soelden – Rettenbachferner –
Tiefenbachferner*
Open: May-December.
Ötztal glaciers road.

Thiersee – Landl – Ackernalm
Open: summer only.
Cars and mini-buses only.

Waidring - Steinplatte Mountain Road

Weer - Nafingersee - Weidener Huette
(or Weer-Saga Alm)

Zell am Ziller (see Zillertal road)

Zillertal Mountain Road
(Hippach - Zellberg - Aschau -
Kaltenbach -Ried)
Open: mid-June-end September.

East Tirol

Iselberg - Zwischenbergen
Open: summer only.

Iselsberg - Roaner Alm
Open: June-mid-October

Kals - Glockner Road
(Kals - Koednitztal)
Toll-free in winter

Lienz - Thurn - Zettersfeld

*Matrei in Osttirol - Matreier Tauernhaus
-Innergschloess*
Up to 9am and from 5pm use limited.
Only passable in summer. Only single-
track vehicles, cars and minibuses.

*St Jacob in Defereggen - Erisbach -
Oberhausalm*
Open: June-September only
Only single-track vehicles and cars.

Thal - Assling - Hochstein Road
(Bannberg Café - Bannberger Alpe)
Open: all year.

Tristach - Kreithof - Dolomitenhuette
Open: mid-May-early October.

MUSEUMS

Note that *Heimatmuseum* is a local
museum.

Innsbruck
Hofkirche, Hofburg, Silbern Kappelle
(Imperial Palace with church and silver
chapel.) Universitats strasse.
Open: May-September, 9am-5pm;
October-April, 9am-12 noon and 2-5pm.
English brochure available.

Tiroler Volkskunstmuseum
(Folk art and crafts)
Next to the Hofkirche.
Open: weekdays 9am-12 noon and
2-5pm, Sundays and holidays 9am-12
noon.
English brochure available.

Landesmuseum Ferdinandeum
15 Museum Strasse.
Open: May-September, weekdays 9am-
5pm, Sundays and holidays 9am-
12.30pm.
A museum of fine arts.

The Armoury
In the Zeughausgasse.
Open: daily 9am-5pm. Closed in winter
A historical museum.

Kaiserjager Museum
On the Bergisel.
Open: May-September, weekdays
9am-4pm.
History of the Tyrolean Imperial elite
mountain regiment 1816 to 1918.

Kaiserschutzen Museum
In Schloss Ambros.
Open: mid-June-September, daily
2-6pm.
Paintings and other souvenirs of the
Imperial Rifle Regiments during World
War I.

Alpine Association Museum
Wilhelm-Greil-Strasse 15.
Open: June-September, Monday-
Friday, 9am-12 noon and 2-5pm.

Kitzbühel
Heimatmuseum
Near town centre.
Open: 9am-12 noon. Closed Sundays
and holidays.
Collection of objects of interest
concerning the town's origins which date
back for 1,000 years.

Kuftstein
Heimatmuseum
Housed in the fortress.
Open: April-October, daily except
Mondays, 9am-6pm. Guided tours in
English take 1¼ hours for the whole
fortress, start at 9.30am, 11am, 1.45pm,
3.15pm and 4.45pm.
Local interest plus illustrations of the
development of the fortress.

Lienz
Osttiroler Heimatmuseum
Housed in Bruck Castle *Schloss Bruck* at

the end of the Schlossgasse.
Open: Easter-October, 10am-5pm.

Schwaz
Heimatmuseum
Housed in Schloss Freundsberg on the
south-eastern outskirts of the town.
Open: mid-April-mid-September, daily,
9am-5pm.

Smaller village museums, easy to find

Alpbach
Open: daily except Tuesdays,
10am-12 noon and 1-5pm.
Mountain farming museum.

Fulpmes
Open: Tuesday and Friday 4-6pm,
Sunday 10am-12 noon.
Forge museum, exhibition of old tools.

Hall in Tyrol
Hasegg Castle.
Open: mid-June-September. Guided
tours at 9.45am, 10.45am, 2.30pm,
3.30pm, 4.30pm, mining museum 10am
and 11am and hourly 2-5pm.
Town museum and mining museum.

Imst
Open: July and August, Monday,
Wednesday and Friday, 9am-12 noon,
and 3-5pm.
Local museum.

Jochberg
Open: Tuesday and Thursday, 5-7pm,
Sunday 10am-12 noon.
Local and mining museum

Landeck
Open: May-September, 10am-5pm.
Landeck Castle museum

Mariastein
Small castle museum. Visits by
arrangement at the tourist office.

Nassereith
Local museum open by arrangement at the council offices.

Nauders
At Nauders fortress.
Open: mid-May-mid-October. Guided tours of the castle Sunday 10am-5pm, tours of the museum on Wednesday, Saturday, and Sunday at 2pm.

St Anton am Arlberg
Open: all day in summer.
Ski and folk museum. History of skiing in the Arlberg region.

Stans
Tratzberg Castle.
Open: Easter-August.
Guided tours daily 10am-3pm

Volders
Friedberg Castle
Open: Guided tours mid-June-mid-September, Wednesday 4pm.
Historic collection, frescoes.

Wildschonau
Open: July-August, daily, except Monday, 10am-12 noon, and 3-5pm; June and September, Saturday and Sunday, 3-5pm.
Museum of alpine farming, in Oberau fire brigade building.

CASTLES

Ambrass,
Innsbruck. South-east outskirts of the city. Just off the minor road to Aldrans.
Open: May-September, 10am-4pm, closed Tuesdays.

Bruck Castle Museum,
Leinz. North-west of town via the

Schlossgasse.
Open: Easter-October, 10am-5pm.

Freundsberg,
Schwaz. South-east of the town near the church.
Open: April-October, 10am-4pm.

Itter
Tenth-century castle, now a hotel.

Kufstein
Open: April-October, 9am-5pm.

Mariastein
Visits by arrangement.

Matzen, Brixlegg
Privately owned; grounds only open.

Nauders
Open: mid-May-mid-October.
Naudersberg Castle museum

Tratzberg,
Jenbach, A6130 Schwaz. Off the minor road between Jenbach and Stans.
Tel: 52422284.

Volders,
Freidberg Castle.
Guided tours, mid-June-mid-September, Wednesday at 4pm.

Two castles at Schwangau, in Germany, but near Reutte.

RUINED CASTLES

Ehrenberg
Reutte. Open any time.

Kropfberg
near Rieth im Alpbachtal.
Imposing site dating from 1200, with three towers.

Nauders
Finstermünz. Ruin of customs fort, fifteenth century.

Rattenberg
Schlossberg.

Kronburg
Zams near Landeck.
Extensive ruin, fourteenth and sixteenth century.

GARDENS

Innsbruck
Bergisel
Off the Brenner road.
Always open.

Hopfgarten
Always open.
Public gardens.

University Botanical Gardens.
Main entrance from the Botanikerstrasse.
Open: daily 7.30am-7pm.

Botanical show in the small Hofgarten. Starting summer 1984. Renweg at the corner of Kapfererstrasse.

Reutte, Alpine.
Reached via the Reutte cable car, the Reuttener Bergbahn, 1 mile south-west of Reutte, near Höfen.
Tel: 45672 2420.

CHURCHES OF SPECIAL NOTE

This is very much a personal choice, as many other beautiful and interesting churches exist in many villages.

Erpfendorf, modern 1957

Hall in Tyrol, parish church, fourteenth century.

Hall in Tyrol, Damenstift (Ladies Abbey), sixteenth century.

Hall in Tyrol, Stiftplatz, ecclesiastical buildings.

Heilingenblut, parish church.

Innsbruck, Cathedral of St James, built in 1717-22.

Innsbruck, Imperial Chapel.

Innsbruck, Wilten Abbey Church, seventeenth century.

Innsbruck, Wilten Basilica of Our Lady of the Four Columns.

Kitzbühel, Church of Our Lady, dating from 1490, but converted in 1730 to Baroque.

Lienz, parish church

Schwaz, Franciscan Cloisters

Schwaz, parish church of the Assumption of Our Blessed Lady. The largest Gothic hall-church of the Tyrol, fifteenth century.

Stams, monastery. Still a partly-walled monastery settlement.

Volders, Servites Church, seventeenth century.

OTHER PLACES OF INTEREST

Lech Falls, near Fussen in Germany.

Plane trips round the Alps from Reutte.

Summer bobsleigh runs at Biberweir and St John in Tyrol.

Pontlatzer Bridge Memorial.

Seventeenth-century inn, Umhausen.

Stuiben Falls, Umhausen.

Stams Monastery.

Ehnbach Klamm, near Zirl.

Bergisel, Innsbruck.

Glass Workshops, Rattenberg.

Krimml Falls.

Albin Egger-Lienz Gallery, Lienz.

Folk Theatre, Reith in Alpbachtal.

Erl. Passion play theatre. Guided tours daily June-September, 2-4pm.

Tuxertal. Watermill in Lanersbach-Juns. Dating from 1839. Put into operation every Monday at 1pm.

Jenbach to Achensee steam train.

Zell am Ziller to Mayrhofen steam train, operates June to September. Visitors have an opportunity to drive the train.

Zoos

Aurach, Wildlife Park.
Five miles south of Kitzbühel on the 161 road then through Oberaurach 4km up the valley. Bus service.
Open: daily 9am-5pm.

Innsbruck, Alpine Zoo.
In the Hungerberg area. Easily reached on foot in 30 minutes. Bus service from the town centre.
Open: daily 9am-6pm.

Swimming

Almost every village has either an indoor or outdoor pool. Many hotels allow visitors into their pools.
The following natural lakes have swimming facilities. Many of them have changing cubicles, sun lawn, recreational areas, boat hire, fishing, restaurants, etc. The water temperature can reach 24-7°C in summer.

Achensee
Largest and loveliest of Tyrol's lakes. Bathing facilities at Pertisau, Maurach-Buchau, Achenkirch, Gaisalm, Maurach and Seespitz.

Frauensee
Near Lechaschau

Holdensee
Between Grän and Nesselwängle in the Tannheimer valley.

Hechtsee
Near Kuftstein

Heiterwangersee
Connected by canal to the Plansee, Tyrol's second largest lake.

Hintersteinersee
Near Scheffau

Krummsee and Reintaltersee
Near Kramsach. Numerous little bays.

Lansersee
On the eastern plateau above Innsbruck.

Lanchsee
South of Fieberbrunn. High sulphur and peat content (up to 26°C).

Nattersee
Between Natters and Goetzens. Peaty water.

Piburgersee
Near Oetz. One of the warmest lakes (up to 24°C) amid dense woods.

Plansee
Near Reutte, surrounded by imposing mountains and lovely woods.

Reithersee
In the centre of Reith in the Alpbach Valley.

Schwarzsee
Near Kitzbühel. Warmest peat-water lake in the Tyrol (up to 27°C).

Seefelder Wildsee
Surrounded by the magnificent scenery of the Wetterstein, Mieminger and Karwendel ranges.

Stimmersee and Hechtsee
Near Kufstein.

Thiersee
North of Kufstein, surrounded by meadows and mountains.

Tristacher See (East Tyrol)
In dense woods at the foot of the Lienzer Dolomites, south of Lienz.

Urisee
East of Reutte, surrounded by woods.

Walchsee
North of the Kaiser Mountains.

SPORT

There are numerous sports facilities in the Tyrol, too many to list individually. Almost all resorts will have facilities for such sports as tennis and bowling.

There is summer skiing at:
Hintertux, Zillertal
Hochgurgl, Ötztal
Kaunertal
Pitztal
Stubaital

There are over seventy horse riding stables in the Tyrol which give lessons for beginners, riding excursions, cross-country rides, etc. Many have accommodation. Further details from the Austrian National Tourist Office.

Golf Courses

Innsbruck, eighteen hole and nine hole. Reached by car via Igls.
A6074, Rinn.
Tel: 05223 8177.
Kitzbühel, nine hole.
A6370, Kitzbühel.
Tel: 05356 3070.
Pertisau, nine hole.
A6213, Pertisau.
Tel: 05243 5377.

Seefeld in Tyrol, eighteen hole.
A6100, Seefeld.
Tel: 05212 3003.
St Johann in Tyrol, nine or eighteen hole.

MOUNTAINEERING SCHOOLS, MOUNTAIN AND SKIING GUIDES

Hochgebirgsschule Tirol
Nairz Wolfgang, A6020 Innsbruck, Anichstrasse 34.

Alpinschule Innsbruck
Gasser Hannes, A6020 Innsbruck, Egger - Lienz - Strasse 130.

Bergsteigerschule Piz Buin-Silvretta
Walter Hugo, A6563 Galtuer Nr 74a.

Alpinschule Ausserfern
Paulweber Sepp, A6600 Reutte, Allgaeuerstrasse 15.

Berg- und Wanderschule Sepp Kroell — Kitzbühel
Kroell Sepp, A6370 Kitzbühel, Floriangasse 7.

Berg- und Wanderschule Kirchdorf am Wilden Kaiser
Birchler Adolf, A6382 Kirchdorf Nr 556.

Alpin- und Bergschule Stubai
Fankhauser Maximilian, A6167 Neustift Nr 107.

Bergschule Tannheimertal
Feuerstein Franz. A6600 Lechaschau.

Alpin- und Wanderschule Zillertal
Habeler Peter, A6290 Mayrhofen Nr 119.

Hochgebirgs- und Wanderschule Obergurgl
Ciacomelli Karl, A6450 Obergurgl.

Alpin- und Wanderschule St Anton a.A.
Strolz Walter, A6580 St Anton a. A. Nr 79.

Bergsteigner- und Bergwanderschule Wetterstein
Wagner Helmut, A6410 Telfs, Am, Kreuzacker 10.

Hochalpine Bergsteigerschule Soelden
Gstrein Martin, A6450 Soelden, Windau Nr 153.

Hochgebirgsschule Innerpitztal
Auer Franz, A6481 St Leonhard im Pitztal, Neurur Nr 97.

Bergsportschule Kaisergebirge
Franz Josef, A6353 Going, Sonnseite 187.

Alpin- und Wanderschule Kitzbühel
Brandstaetter Peter, A6370 Kitzbühel, Aschbachweg 15.

Wander- und Hochgebirgsschule Fulpmes/Stubai und Wipptal
Rettenbacher Josef, A6166 Fulpmes, Groebenweg 11.

Hochgebirgs- und Wanderschule Tuxertal
Tomann Anton, A6293 Lannersbach Nr 361.

Wander- und Hochgebirgsschule Fieberbrunn
Trixl Leonhard, A6391 Fieberbrunn, Koglehen 37.

Alpinsportschule Alpbachtal
Lintner Josef, A6236 Alpbach Nr 247.

Alpin- und Wanderschule Ehrwald-Zugspitze
Scheiber Kurt, A6632 Ehrwald Hoelzi 13.

Aplin-und Wanderschule Achensee
Hausberger Ludwig, A6212 Maurach, Buchau Nr 57b.

Alpinschule Hochpustertal
Sint Josef, A9941 Kartitsch Nr 17.

Berg- und Wanderschule Ellmau am Wilden Kaiser
Fuerstaller Sebastian, A6352 Ellmau, Sonnseite 148.

St Johann I.T.
Opening of a mountaineering school is planned for summer 1984.

Bergsteigerschule des Österreichen Alpenvereins
A6020 Innsbruck, Wilhelm-Greil-Strasse.

Touristenverein
'Die Naturfreunde', A6020 Innsbruck, Salurnerstrasse 1.

The Tyroleon Tourist Board will be pleased to supply special brochures regarding Mountaineering Schools and their programmes, mountain refuges and Alpine inns. These include suggestions for rambles and a list of Tyroleon mountain and skiing guides.

CYCLE HIRE

Cycles may be hired at:

Axams
Ebbs
Kössen
Langenfeld
Lienz
Zell am Ziller

WATER SPORTS

Sailing

Sailing School Achensee, A6215, Achenkirch.
Sailing Club Achensee, A6212, Buchau bei Maurach am Achensee.
Sailing Club Plansee, A6600, Reutte.
Sailing School Durlassboden Reservoir, A6281, Gerlos.

Further information may be obtained from the local Tourist Offices or from the Tiroler Wasser sportverein

(Tyrolean Water Sports Association),
A6020, Innsbruck, Franz-Fisher Strasse
23.

Surfing

Surfing School Achensee, Dora Storm,
St Hubertus Inn, A6213, Pertisau.
Sailing and Surfing School Achensee,
Friedrich Schwaiger, Seeblick Inn,
A6215, Achenkirch.
Surfing School Durlassboden Reservoir,
Tourist Office Gerlos, A6281, Gerlos.
Surfing School Groen-Haldensee,
Sportsclub Montanara, Sport hotel,
Rot-Flush, A6673, Haldensee.
Surfing School Pillersee, Heinz Mueller,
Pfarrau 19a, A6370, Kitzbühel.
Surfing School Plansee, Arnold
Winklmair, Hotel Forelle, A6600,
Reutte.
Surfing School Walchsee-Kössen, Sport
Merkl, department store Payr, A6345,
Kössen.

Surfing is allowed on the following
lakes:

Achensee, permits from Tourist Offices
in Pertisau and Achenkirch.
Plansee, permits from Hotel Seespitze
and Hotel Forelle in Reutte.
Heiterwangersee.
Haldensee.
Durlassboden Reservoir.
Hintersteinersee.
Thiersee, permits from the bathing
place.
Walsee, permits from the Surfing School
(address above).

On Schwarzsee near Kitzbühel and
Tristachersee near Tristach in East
Tirol, surfing is limited to after 5pm and
only if swimmers are not disturbed.
Permits from Schwarzsee bathing place
and Hotel Tristachersee.

Canoeing

Canoeing is possible on a number of
rivers in the Tyrol. Further information
from the Tyrolean Water Sports
Association (address above).

White Water Sports

White water courses, May-mid-
September, in the Zemm gorge in
Mayrhofen.
Information from Michael
Platzgummer, Hauptstrasse 446, A6290,
Mayrhofen.

Water Skiing

Schwarzsee, near Kitzbühel. Electrically
driven circular course.
Walchsee.

Motor Boats

Motor boats with internal combustion
engines prohibited on all Tyrolean lakes;
electric engines permitted to a maximum
capacity of 500 watt.

Fishing

Fishing is possible at many resorts.
Details from Austrian National Tourist
Office, or local Tourist Offices.

ACTIVITY HOLIDAYS

Alpbach. Woodcarving, stained glass.
Elbigenalp. Woodcarving.
Ellmau. Bread making, Tyrolean
specialities, bouquet making.
Imst. Handicrafts (silk painting,
painting in peasant style, macramé,
flower arrangements, etc).
Innsbruck. German language courses for
foreigners, German literature, Austrian-
German culture.
Jungholz. Woodcarving.

Kirchberg. Painting in peasant style.
Kitzbühel. Deutsch-Institut Tirol
(German Institute Tyrol).
Kufstein. Handicrafts (drawing,
painting, enamel work, modelling,
pottery, woodcarving, block printing).
Lechaschau. Handloom weaving.
Leutasch. Various courses.
Mayrhofen. German language for
foreigners. Steam engine trips for
amateur engine men on the Zillertal
train. Song recitals.
Obenberg. Painting.
Pettnau am Arlberg. Woodcarving.
Rettenschoess. Accordion playing.
St Johann in Tirol. Bread making,
household remedies, natural cuisine.
Sautens. Painting in peasant style.
Serfaus. Archery.
Soelden. Tyrolean cooking, local
dialects, painting, photography, etc.
Tannheim. Handloom weaving. Painting
in peasant style.
Weer-Kolsass-Kolsassberg. Variety of
organised sports.
Weissenbach. Root carving.
Westendorf. German language courses.

Further details from Austrian National
Tourist Office or local Tourist Offices.

CAMPSITES

This list includes top-grade sites with full
facilities, such as showers, shops and
restaurants. Many other sites exist. (E)
denotes English spoken.

Achenkirch. H. Geisler, Camping
Achensee,A6215, Achenkirch 17.
Tel: 5246 6329
Achenkirch. Kogler, Camping
Fichtenwald, A6215, Achenkirch 558.
Tel: 5246 6387
Aschau im Zillertal. A. u. H. Fiegl,
Camping Aufenfeld, A6274, Distelberg

Nr 1.
Tel: 5282/2916 (E)
Biberwier. Camping Biberhof, A6633.
Tel: 5673 2950 (E)
Brixen im Thale. Camping platz Brixen
im Thale, A6364.
Tel: 5334 8113 (E)
Buch im Inntal. R. Feix,
Rennhammergasse 16, 6130, Schwaz
Tel: 5242 48762.
Ehrwald. Camping-caravaning-platz der
Tiroler Zugspitzebahn, A6632.
Tel: 5673 2745 (E)
Ehrwald. Internationaler Campingplatz,
Dr Lauth, A6632.
Tel: 5673 2666 (E)
Fieberbrunn. Tirol.-Camp, A6391,
Lindau 20.
Tel: 5354 6666 (E)
Fügen. A. Hell, Camping Zillertal,
A6263, Fügen 212.
Tel: 5288 2203
Grän-Haldensee. B. Huber, A6673,
Haldensee (E)
Grän-Haldensee. Rudolf Gehring,
A6673, Grän 34
Tel: 5675 6570.
Haiming. Camping-Centre Oberland,
A6430.
Tel: 5266 294 (E)
Hall in Tirol. Herbert Niedrist,
Scheidensteinstrasse 24, A6060.
Tel: 5223 734528 (E)
Häselgehr. Rudolf Riedmann, A6651.
Tel: 5634 6425 (E)
Heiterwang. Hotel Fisher am See, A6611
Tel: 5674 5116 (E)
Hopfgarten im Brixental. A. Reiterhof,
Penningberg 90, A6361.
Tel: 5335 2490 (E)
Imst (oberstadt). Böss, Engrerweg 5,
A6460.
Tel: 5412 2866 (E)
Imst (west). F. Fink, Langgase 30,
A6460.
Tel: 5412 3364 (E)
Imst. International Campingplatz beim

Schwimmbad, (near the pool), A6460.
Tel: 5412 2612 (E)
Innsbruck. Campingplatz, Innsbruck-west, A6020.
Tel: 5222 84180 (E)
Innsbruck-Amras. Gasthaus Seewirt, A6020 (Geyr Strasse).
Tel: 5222 46153 (E)
Innsbruck-Reichenau. Alois Saska, A6020 (near the river, Reichenaur strasse).
Tel: 5222 46252 (E)
Itter. J ager, Itter 140, A6300, (Schlossber Itter).
Tel: 5335 2181 (E)
Jungholz. Eugen Lochbihler, A6691.
Tel: 5676 882 (E)
Kaltenbach. J. Geisler, Kaltenbach Nr 3, A6272.
Tel: 5283 2290
Kaunertal-Feichten. Camping Kaunertal, Familie Hafele, Ortsteil Platz im Kaunertal, A6524.
Tel: 5475 316 (E)
Kitzbühel. Campingplatz Schwarzsee, A6370.
Tel: 5356 2806 (E)
Kössen. Eurocamp Wilder Kaiser, A6345.
Tel: 5375 6444 (E)
Kramsach. A. Brunner, Kramsach 23, A6233 (Seeblick-Toni).
Tel: 5337 3544
Kramsach. G. Sappl, Kramsach 481, A6233 (Stadlerhof).
Tel: 5337 28065.
Kramsach. P. Brunner, Moosen 21, A6233 (Seehof).
Tel: 5337 3541
Kufstein. Camping Kufstein, Gasthof Bären, A6330.
Tel: 5372 3689
Ladis. Max Senn, Ladis 60, A6531.
Tel: 5472 6607 (E)
Landeck. J. Huber, (Camping West), A6500.
Tel: 5442 2324 (E)

Landeck. Schimpfösl, Bruggfeldstrasse 2, A6500 (Riffler).
Tel: 5442 39405 (E)
Längenfeld. A. Kuprain, Huben Nr 117, A6444.
Tel: 5253 5591 (E)
Längenfeld. Camping Ötztal, Ferdinand Aver, Unterlangenfeld 7, A6444.
Tel: 5252 5348 (E)
Längenfeld. S. Kneisl, Winkle Nr 38, A6444.
Tel: 5253 5591 (E)
Langkampfen. Hager KG, Au 326, 6330 Kufstein, A6322.
Tel: 5372 4390
Lermoos. Camping Hofherr, Garmischer Strass 21, A6631.
Tel: 5673 2980 (E)
Lermoos. W. Schonger, Gries Nr 16, A6631.
Tel: 5673 2197 (E)
Maurach. Peppo Loinger, Muarach 115a, A6212.
Tel: 5243 5297 (E)
Maurach-Bachau. A. Wimmer, Buchau 136, A6212.
Tel: 5243 5217 (E)
Mayrhofen. Josef Kröll, Mayrhofen 127, A6290.
Tel: 5285 2580
Mils bei Hall in Tirol. Gasthof Milser Brücke, Bunderstrasse Nr 7, A6060.
Tel: 5223 6360 (E)
Nassereith. Hotel Schloss, Fernsteinsee, A6465.
Tel: 5265 5210 (E)
Nassereith. Rainer Ruepp, Rossbach 325, A6465.
Tel: 5265 5426 (E)
Natters. Ing Giner, Natterer See Nr 1, A6162. Tel: 5222 23988 (E)
Neustift. Hans Pfurtscheller, Neustift Nr 97, A6167.
Tel: 5226 2517 (E)
Neustift. Müllerhof, Hermann Pfurtscheller, Neustift Nr 115, A6167.
Tel: 5226 2537 (E)

Ötz. H. Jäger, A6433.
Tel: 5252 6485   (E)
Pettnau. H. Köll, Camping Leiblfing,
A6020.
Tel: 5238 8264
Pfunds. Hotel Sonne, E. Habicher,
A6542.
Tel: 5474 5232   (E)
Pill bei Schwaz. Gasthof Plankenhof,
A6130.
Tel: 5242 4195.
Prutz. A. Senn, Prutz Nr 55, A6522
(Sauerbrunnplatz).
Tel: 5472 6267
Reutte. Camping Forelle, A6600.
Tel: 5672 8115   (E)
Reutte. Camping Seespitze, A6600.
Tel: 5672 8121   (E)
Reutte. J. Lechner, A6600 (Am
Sintwag).
Tel: 5672 2809   (E)
Ried im Oberinntal. K. Patscheider, Reid
41, A6531.
Tel: 5472 6571   (E)
Rinn. Gemeindeamt Rinn, A6074.
Tel: 5223 8110
St Jodok am Brenner. O. Renzler, Wolf
33, A6154 (Wolf).
Tel: 5279 325
St Johann in Tyrol. Gasthof Michlhof,
A6380.
Tel: 5352 2584   (E)
Scharnitz. Kluckner Karl, Camping
Alm, A6108.
Scheffau. E. Mühlberger, Blaiken 74,
A6351.
Tel: 5358 8149
Schönweis. A. Staggl, Schönweis 21,
A6491.
Tel: 5418 5209
Schwoich. S. Maier, Egerbach 54,
A6330.
Tel: 5372 8352
Sölden. Camping Sölden, A6450.
Tel: 5254 2627   (E)
Stams. M. Kluibenschedl, Stams 66,
A6422, (Eichenwald).

Tel: 5263 6458   (E)
Telfs. Rattacher, Wassertal 1, A6410
(West).
Tel: 5262 31223
Telfs. Scharmer, A6410 (near the
swimming pool).
Tel: 5262 2849
Thiersee. A. Messner, Haisenhof, A6335.
Tel: 5376 258
Thiersee. J. Atzl, Rueppenhof, A6335.
Tel: 5376 419
Umhausen. Karl Falkner, Alpencamping
Falkner, A6441.
Tel: 5255 5203
Unterperfuss. Georg Hörtnagl,
Unterperfuss Nr 32, A6175 (Farm
Camp).
Tel: 5232 2209
Volders. Altenburger, A6111
(Castlecamping).
Tel: 5224 2333   (E)
Vols. M. Stigger, Bahnhofstrasse 10,
A6176.
Tel: 5222 322344   (E)
Waidring. K. Hechenblaiker, A6384.
Tel: 5353 5345   (E)
Walchsee. Bad Seemühle, A6344
(Seemühle).
Tel: 5374 5458   (E)
Walchsee. Camping Seespitz, Postfach
12, A6344 (Seespitz).
Tel: 5374 5359   (E)
Walchsee. G. Grünbacher, A6344
(Terrace camping South Lake).
Tel: 5374 5339   (E)
Weer. E. Mark, A6114 (Alpen
Camping).
Tel: 5224 8146   (E)
Westendorf. Panorama-Camping-
Freihof, Mühltal, A6363.
Tel: 5334 6166   (E)
Wiesing. J. Brugger, A6220. (Inntal
Camping).
Tel: 5244 2693
Zams. Wachtler Edith, Magdalenweg 1,
A6511.
Tel: 5442 3289   (E)

Zell am Ziller. G. Hofer, Gerlosstrasse 33, A6280.
Tel: 5282 2248   (E)
Zirl. J. Ruepp, Eigenhofen, A6170.
Tel: 5238 27204   (E)
Zirl. J. Stroll, Mühlgasse 19, A6170.
Tel: 5238 2398   (E)

EAST TYROL

Debant bei Lienz. Gasthof Dolomitenrast, A9900.
Tel: 4852 2447
Leisach. J. Zanon, Gasthof Südalpen, A9900.
Tel: 4852 3327
Lienz. Gasthof Falken, Eichholz A9900.
Tel: 4852 4022   (E)
Lienz. Gasthof Glocknerhof, A9900.
Tel: 4852 2167
Lienz. Nogler, Iseltaler Strasse, A9900 (Sun Valley).
Tel: 4852 3163   (E)
Matrei im Osttirol. Steiner, Edenweg 15, A9971.
Tel: 4875 6679
Prägraten. W. Unterwurzacher, Prägraten 73, A9974 (Venediger-Camping).
Tel: 4877 213
Prägraten. Anna Dorer, Hinterbichl 9a, A9974.
Tel: 4877 223
Tristach. Pension Camping Seeweise, A9900.
Tel: 4852 3907.

Götzens, Kirchstrasse
Tel: 5234 8556
Innsbruck, Reichenauer Strasse 147
Tel: 5222 46179
Innsbruck, Sillgasse 8a
Tel: 5222 31311

Innsbruck, Rennweg 17b
Tel: 5222 25814
Kaltenbach/Stumm, Stummerberg 68
Kufstein, SchlassHohenstaffing
Tel: 5372 52514
Lienz, Zetterfeld
Tel: 4852 4302
Lienz, Linker Iselweg
Tel: 4852 3310
Reutte-Höfen, Postfach 3
Tel: 5672 2644
Wildshönau-Oberau, Mülhtal 76
Tel: 5339 815194

VISITOR'S TICKETS

Reductions on various charges are available at a large number of resorts in the Tyrol. Enquire at local Tourist Offices for further information.

FACILITIES FOR CHILDREN

Many of the larger resorts have kindergartens for visitor's children, while a number of villages have a baby-sitter servicè; many hotels can supervise children throughout the day. Special activities for children are organised by many resorts, such as parties, picnics, rambles, competitions, games, swimming, barbecues, sports, farm visits etc. Basic details may be obtained from the Austrian National Tourist Office, while details of dates and times are obtainable from local Tourist Offices.

ALPINE FLIGHTS

Special tourist flights around the Tyrol are available from Innsbruck Airport. The flights last 60, 40 or 30 minutes and may be booked at short notice. They give spectacular views of the city, mountains, valleys and towns.

McCarta Ltd, (maps)
122 Kings Cross Road,
London.
Tel: 01 278 8278

Austrian Alpine Club, (maps)
13 Longcroft House,
Fretherne Road,
Welwyn Garden City,
Herts.
Tel: 07073 24835

Austrian National Tourist Office,
30 St George Street,
London.
Tel: 01 629 0461

Ramblers Association
1/5 Wandsworth Road,
London SW8 2LJ
Tel: 01 582 6878

Youth Hostels Association,
Trevelyan House,
St Stephens Hill,
St Albans,
Herts AL1 2DY
Tel: 0727 55215

Österreicher Jugendherbergsverband,
(Austrian Youth Hostels Association),
A1010 Vienna,
Schottenring 28,
Austria
Tel: 222 635353

Rand McNally Map Store,
10 E 53rd Street,
New York, New York.

American Youth Hostels Association,
75 Spring Street,
New York, New York.

Austrian National Tourist Office,
500 5th Avenue,
New York, New York.

Index

139

144